FIRESIDE

Growing
Herbs in Pots

TEXT AND ILLUSTRATIONS BY

JOHN BURTON BRIMER

A FIRESIDE BOOK
PUBLISHED BY SIMON AND SCHUSTER

Copyright © 1976 by John B. Brimer
All rights reserved
including the right of reproduction
in whole or in part in any form
A Fireside Book
Published by Simon and Schuster
A Division of Gulf & Western Corporation
Simon & Schuster Building
Rockefeller Center
1230 Avenue of the Americas
New York, New York 10020
FIRESIDE and colophon are registered trademarks
of Simon & Schuster

Manufactured in the United States of America

3 4 5 6 7 8 9 10 11

Library of Congress Cataloging in Publication Data

Brimer, John Burton.
Growing herbs in pots.

Includes index.
1. Herb gardening.   2. Container gardening.
3. Cookery (Herbs)   I. Title.
SB351.H5B66   635'.7   76-2529
ISBN 0-671-22252-X
ISBN 0-671-24207-5 Pbk.

Contents

I
About Herbs

1·Herbs—Fragrant, Piquant, Poetic

Although it may seem as if culinary herbs, which are so widely used today, had been a part of our European cooking heritage from the beginning of time, this is not quite the case. In northern Europe they appeared rather late, carried there from various parts of the world that were more advanced. At first herbs were planted and treasured, but as their use increased they escaped the gardens and naturalized themselves wherever favorable soils were found. The Romans, conquering *Gallia omnis,* carried along their favored herbs, which included onions and garlic. And when the barbarians drove them back into Italy they left behind their important contributions to gastronomy.

Returning Crusaders introduced from the East many of those herbs so esteemed in French cookery today. Along with gold and other material booty they carried home seeds and roots of herb plants—anise, scallions, shallots, and thyme—as well as packets of many aromatic spices, all of which they had acquired a taste for while indulging in Eastern foods. Since most spices could not be grown in the West, trade routes were soon established for the importation of ginger, cinnamon, and pepper, and probably some herbs traveled this route too. The prices of the imports reflected the labor involved and matched the length of the journeys. In fact, common black pepper was once such an exotic condiment that "costly as pepper" was an ancient byword. Land-rent agreements often specified annual payment of a certain number of peppercorns in place of—or in addition to—actual money. But herbs, fortunately, were cheap and easy to grow, so that their use spread widely.

As life became more agreeable and communications improved, herb seeds and roots became accepted flavoring ingredients that were experimentally added to many old recipes. Cooks in noble houses and rich merchants' kitchens vied with each other in concocting new dishes. Often these involved fanciful or exotic uses of herbs. Rich honors might be bestowed upon the host by a king, a duke, or other overlord if he were pleased by some unusual dish. All through the Middle Ages an inordinate degree of attention was paid to food, according to old chronicles, by the nobles and the rich, even though peasants and commoners might be close to starvation outside the walls of the castles, manors, and town houses.

About the year 1330—the time the Valois became rulers of France—fabulous banquets began to be recorded in histories of the time. It was later that these spread to other parts of Europe and to Britain. Herbs were working their way into every national cuisine in Europe. In the Orient, of course, they had long been established as integral parts of recipes. By the time Catherine de Médici became queen of France, the national cuisine was secure enough to add outside influences to the French gustatory delights. Possibly, according to some accounts, certain borrowings came from Italy, but all were soon so integrated into the French cuisine that there is no real proof of their Italian origin and only a historian would quibble over the point.

Earlier, herbs had become so plentiful in many areas that they were dried and mixed together as "strewing herbs" to be scattered on fresh-swept floors of palaces and manor halls. They aided in counteracting the noisome smells of houses where sanitation was, at best, primitive. Even beyond the Tudor era the sweet and pungent aromas of strewing herbs were used to cover somewhat the odors of the "drains" (sewage-disposal systems that did *not* drain) and all the other unpleasant waftings of life of those times.

By the late nineteenth century the *haute cuisine* of France, with its elegant and elaborate recipes, was world famous. In the provinces a simpler sort of cookery prevailed, and it was probably here that the hard-pressed cooks evolved the *bouquets garnis* and the *fines herbes* combinations as a means of adding flavor to many dishes. Today we also incline to the simpler approach, favoring recipes that do not require lengthy, days-ahead preparation. The aim of most cooks is to enhance the natural flavor of foods, not to dominate them with highly flavored sauces and dressings. Properly used, herbs not only make the lesser cuts of meat palatable but also bring out the fine flavors of choice cuts. Herbs are welcome additives to many vegetable recipes too, and now that we have year-round supplies of fresh foods, thanks to transportation and refrigeration, we also can grow year-round fresh herbs to use with them. Ancient cooks would be popeyed at the treasures at our disposal. The world, so to speak, is our oyster—and not only because we may now eat oysters all year, not just in R months.

You should grow your own herbs to get the fullest flavor. Buying packaged ones may mean flavor loss by being dried commercially, or their aromas and flavors may evaporate from cardboard boxes. Even in sealed bottles some deterioration takes place if the herbs are kept too long. And there is no way of determining exactly how long they have rested on shop shelves or in storage. Growing your own herbs means always having them fresh on hand, and when you produce a surplus, they can be dried or frozen against a lean time. You will know, of course, exactly how long they have been preserved. You will also enjoy

11

a more intimate connection with your herbs when they are grown in containers rather than en masse in outdoor beds. All culinary herbs have an innate beauty as well as down-to-earth utilitarian uses, and many make interesting houseplants.

With modern growing techniques, success is more certain now, whether herbs are grown in a sunny window or with artificial light. Contact with green, growing plants is a spur to creativity, to experimentation in the use of herbs to vary standard recipes. The recipes in this book may be used as guidelines that will suggest other uses to creative cooks. Beginners or cooks who lead extra-busy lives may want to use them as they are. But they may suggest ways to add to recipes from other sources. The main point is that fresh herbs are best and everyone can grow them in containers.

2·Success with Herbs Indoors

Fortunately most of the herbs we commonly use in cookery lend themselves quite well to container culture, either indoors or outside, making this an interesting and rewarding hobby. While most herbs do best in sunlight, not all need heat. In fact, almost all indoor plants do best in a cool atmosphere, or at least one cooler than most Americans are accustomed to in their houses. The recent energy crisis brought pleas for lowering temperatures a few degrees, which proved a boon for the indoor gardener. Herbs, too, like a greater amount of humidity than is usually found in our homes—and increased humidity will also benefit the human inhabitants. We need a more humid atmosphere in winter than is usually found indoors, according to authorities on health. If the air is kept more humid we will find that temperatures seem a little higher than the thermometer readings would indicate. Most herbs do best in a range between 50 and 60 degrees F. Where light conditions are poor or during the shorter days of winter, adequate light—a vital necessity for plants—can be supplied by artificial lighting. (See Chapter V.)

The herbs described here should grow well with very little care and nothing much beyond what most other houseplants require. They may be kept indoors all year, or if you have a balcony or terrace, they may be summered outdoors. If you have a house rather than an apartment, a place near the kitchen door will be a convenient spot outdoors for them, and the pots will add a pleasant, decorative note to the back-door steps.

BASIL

Ocimum basilicum

In France cooks often speak of basil as *l'herbe royale*, both because the name stems from a word for "king" in its original Greek form (*basileios*) and because the herb is so regal in taste and use. Amusingly, it was once thought in ancient days to be associated with basilisks, those fabled reptiles whose very look or breath was fatal to humans. But cooks are not concerned with that legend so much as with its use in cookery. And Italian cooks may know that it has been an enduring symbol of love from the time that it grew in the kitchen gardens of old Rome. In India the herb signifies reverence for the dead and it is considered holy. Basil was one of the strewing herbs that were spread on floors in Tudor times in England to add a pleasant smell.

Probably basil came originally from India, moving to Greece and westward across Europe to the British Isles. It arrived in America early in the seventeenth century along with other herbs to enrich the limited diet of Colonial times. Today we know it especially for its association with tomato dishes, particularly for its use in Italian and Spanish recipes. Although it is mild enough when used fresh in tomato salads, tomato juice, and other recipes, such as a shrimp-cocktail sauce, it must be used with discretion when it is to be cooked. It is one of the few herbs that increase in flavor when heated.

It has long been grown successfully in pots, and in France there is a tradition that a pot of basil on restaurant tables outdoors will keep flies away. Also from Europe comes the superstition that basil in the house will keep witches at bay. Since I have never seen any flies on basil, nor have I encountered witches in the vicinity of the plant, I am unable to disprove these rumored effects.

Basil has a sweet scent somewhat like that of tomato plants in hot sun, which emphasizes its affinity for tomatoes in recipes. It makes a handsome, bushy small plant, growing to a foot or more indoors, and it has oval-pointed green leaves. A purple-leaved variety, 'Dark Opal', is decorative and equally useful in cookery. Never allow basil to bloom or the plant will go to seed, and since it is an annual, its day will be over. Pinch out the tip with the thumb and forefinger nails to prevent flowering. This will also keep the plant low and bushy.

Recipes that include Basil are:

Tomato Juice à la Riviera
Tomato Juice Italiano
Tomato and Herb Spread
Herbed Tomato Aspic
Herbal Broth
Soupe au Pistou
Herbed Egg Casserole
Shirred Eggs with Cheese
Tomato and Meatballs
Chicken Cacciatore
Rabbit Braised with Herbs
Pesto alla Genovese
Herb Butter Sauce

Onion-Tomato Sauce
Sauce Rémoulade
Herbed Stewed Tomatoes
*Tomatoes Stuffed with
  Herbed Rice*
Baked Eggplant with Cheese
A Salad of Tossed Greens
*Tomato Salad and Fines
  Herbes*
Bouquets Garnis
Fines Herbes
Herbed Garlic Butter

CHIVE

Allium schoenoprasum

Although the smallest member of the onion family, the chive (or chives, since it is usually referred to in the plural) looms large as an important ingredient in national cuisines the world over. The Chinese cuisine, well established by 3000 B.C., mentions chives in many recipes. The Egyptians also grew them, and we know that, later on, the Romans planted them and as a matter of course took them along on those conquering forays across Europe and probably into England.

It is for the leaves that chives are grown, and they are favorites because they add a mild oniony flavor. Cut, snipped into tiny bits, and sprinkled over cold or hot dishes, they are often combined with other herbs, as in the classic French combinations called *fines herbes*, in which they are one of the four principal ingredients. Chives may also be frozen, either alone or in combination with other herbs. The flavor diminishes when they are dried. However, it is possible to place chive leaves in noniodized salt, keep them there for several weeks, remove the leaves, then bottle the "chive salt" for use in flavoring.

Like those of all onions, the leaves are tubular, growing in clumps from a small bulb and reaching 8 to 12 inches in height. When clumps are divided—as they must be when the pot becomes crowded—the tiny white bulbs left over may be pickled like cocktail onions. Although the fuzzy lavender pompon blooms are appealing to view, the plants lose flavor after blooming, so we should prevent chives from flowering. Outdoors where there is plenty of space, bloom need not be limited and the aesthetic sense can be indulged in garden rows of chives.

Recipes calling for chives are many and various—stews and casseroles benefit from them; finely chopped, they add distinction to omelets and scrambled eggs. Many soups are improved by a few snippings of chives, while for vichyssoise, scattering chopped chives over the surface is mandatory. As a welcome change from parslied boiled potatoes, sprinkle finely chopped chives over boiled new potatoes, or add them to sour cream and serve with baked Idaho potatoes. In salad dressings and salads they add color and flavor. Anywhere that a light oniony flavor is desirable, chives will serve admirably.

Combined with two or more other herbs they will make a real contribution to *bouquets garnis* (see p. 179) and *fines herbes* (p. 180). These combinations may be made up and frozen so that they are instantly available for use.

Recipes that include Chives are:

Tomato and Herb Spread	*Scrambled Eggs with Herbs*
Herb Dip	*Ravigote Butter Sauce*
Herbed Cream Cheese Spread	*Herb Butter Sauce*
Herbal Broth	*Sauce Verte (Green*
Parslied Potato Potage	*Mayonnaise)*
Cucumber and Yoghurt Soup	*Sauce Tartare*
Tuna-Stuffed Eggs with	*Salad of Tossed Greens*
Cucumbers	*Bouquets Garnis*
Ham-Deviled Eggs	*Fines Herbes—Classic*
Ham Omelet with	*Blend*
Cucumbers	

DILL

Anethum graveolens

Although the word "dill" stems from the Anglo-Saxon *dile* or the Medieval English *dille,* meaning "to lull," the plant itself originated in the Mediterranean region, moving eastward and northward. It was much treasured by the Greeks and Romans and it is easy to understand why ancient poets sang songs in its praise. The Greeks favored it as a condiment, among other culinary applications, while the Romans utilized it also in decorating their banquet halls. They made wreaths of it to crown their heroes. Taking seeds along on their conquests of Europe, they planted dill, leaving it as an herbal heritage. Some time or other dill arrived in Scandinavia, where to this moment it is perhaps the most important of culinary herbs, as popular as parsley is elsewhere.

Dill is an annual plant, easily grown from seed, which germinates in ten days to two weeks. Outdoors it grows to about 3 feet, but in pots indoors it will be less tall. The variety 'Dill Bouquet' will be low-growing because it is more dwarf in habit. The George Park Seed Company lists it. Dill needs plenty of sun and a rich soil indoors to perform well, but it will grow under lights all winter long from late-summer plantings. Successive plantings should be made to ensure a continuing crop if you plan to use much of it. The gracefully curving, feathery leaves and the umbrella-shaped flowerhead make it a distinctively decorative plant with a character all its own.

Recipes calling for dill weed refer to the leaves and stems of dill; other recipes may call for the seeds. Excess crops can be dried. Dry dill is less pungent than the fresh leaves, which may be bitter-tasting. Stems are even more bitter. Finely chopped leaves sprinkled over boiled new potatoes or on potato salad, over steaks and chops shortly before taking them from under the broiler for serving, a small quantity added to stews, soups (especially those with a meat base), and to bland vegetables will bring welcome flavor to these foods. Dill butter on fried or broiled fish is also delectable. Some cooks add a few sprigs to boiling water to lessen the fishy smell of cooking shrimp. Snipped dill adds a delightful note to many vegetable dishes, such as lima beans or sliced beets.

Sow seeds in a 10-inch pot, and when plants are well up, thin to four or five sturdy seedlings. Dill does not transplant well, and it needs depth for long taproots. To keep plants growing longer, pinch out the tops to prevent flowering and seed setting.

Recipes that include Dill are:

Cucumber and Yoghurt Soup   *Rhine Wine Sauce*

SWEET MARJORAM

Majorana hortensis

Flavorsome and fragrant, the "herb of happiness," sweet marjoram was fashioned into crowns for newlyweds in ancient Greece and Rome as a symbol of happiness. Today we assure our happiness by its culinary use, for it is a most versatile herb. Often combined with sage and other herbs, it is also sometimes substituted for sage in certain dishes, giving them a less pungent flavor. It formerly had its share of medicinal uses in remedies for an astonishing array of illnesses, among them some found in Gerard's *Herball* of 1597: "Majerone is a remedy against cold diseases of the braine and head, being taken in any way to your best liking. . . . it easeth the tooth-ache being chewed in the mouth." I like best, however, this: "The leaves boiled in water, and the decoction drunke, easeth such as are given to overmuch sighing." Happiness, it would seem, is a sprig of marjoram!

In cookery today it is a major ingredient, usually dried, in poultry seasonings or stuffings, and its use is also standard in sausages, especially British, and in the German *Wurst*. Always welcome in oil dressings for green salads, it combines well with chicken salad too. Try it with seafood chowders, in onion, pea, potato, and tomato soups, and in oyster stew. Rub it inside poultry and small game birds before roasting them, but do not stuff them. Sprinkle pulverized marjoram over meats before roasting them and use finely chopped fresh leaves generously on fish about to be baked. A few fresh leaves in boiling water with peas, lentils, green beans and limas, spinach and zucchini will add a touch of glamour to the vegetables. Finely chopped leaves sprinkled over cooked carrots or mushrooms will give them a new individuality. Add a sprinkling of dried marjoram to cheese and egg dishes and dust it lightly over macaroni and cheese for a new taste in a familiar dish.

Marjoram is closely related to oregano and is often substituted for it, but remember to add more marjoram than the oregano called for in a recipe, for marjoram is much less pungent than oregano. Marjoram is an upright plant growing indoors to about 8 to 12 inches tall, with gray-green leaves and reddish stems. It likes sun and a barely moist soil. Pinching back the tips or harvesting sprigs to use in cooking will keep it bushy and productive. It may be started in the seeding mediums (see Chapter IV) or in the 5-inch pot in which it will grow. The seeds are tiny, so scatter them well; they are slow to germinate. Thin out seedlings to about three to a pot, or perhaps only two if growing conditions are really good. Seedlings may also be transplanted from the seeding medium, and three or four grown in an 8-inch pot.

Recipes that include Marjoram are:

Herbed Egg Casserole
Casserole of Beans au Berger
Herb-Stuffed Roast Rabbit
Rabbit Braised with Herbs
Multi-Herb Sauce
Five-Herb Wine Sauce
Green Beans aux Herbes
Green Beans au Jambon
   Julienne

Dried Black Beans Baked
   with Herbs
A Salad of Tossed Greens
Bouquets Garnis
Fines Herbes, Meat and
   Sauce Blend
Fines Herbes, Meat Blend
Herb Vinegars
Herb Butter

21

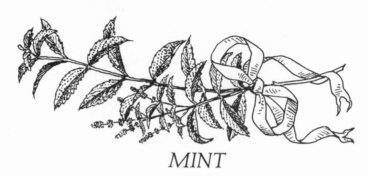

MINT

Mentha species

Gerard in his famous *Herball* of 1597, noting various details concerning mint, began by stating succinctly: "There be divers sorts of Mints, some of the garden, others wilde or of the field; and also some of the water." "Divers" is indeed the word, for there are some twenty species of mint and many varieties, but for our purposes only a few prove to be of culinary use. Fortunately mint may be grown in containers.

Captivating in taste and aroma, mint is unique among herbs in that it flavors everything from appetizers to desserts. In between are enough recipes for other foods to compile a large mint cookbook. Everyone loves mint (not that this is news); it was known ages ago in India and in Egypt, and both Greeks and Romans used it not alone in cookery but also for various symbolic rites. It was so plentiful that in medieval Europe and later it was a strewing herb that scented the floors of banquet halls. By early Christian times its medicinal properties had made it a crop valuable enough for the Church to exact a portion in payment of tithes. In those days everyone used mint as a remedy for headaches (or even for insomnia) by placing leaves on the forehead. And as a digestive it served well. The rich scented their bath waters with oil of mint and enjoyed the herb in many dishes. Although recorded in cookery in the fourteenth century, we suspect it was used in this way throughout the Dark Ages.

22

Certainly the Romans, addicted to its use, took mint roots with them in their travels, leaving a legacy of naturalized plants when they departed.

From the earliest times mint was admired, as recorded in Gerard's *Herball:* "The smell of Mint, saith *Pliny,* doth stir up the minde, and the taste to a greedy desire of meat. Mint is marvellous wholesome for the stomacke." Gourmets today admit the mere thought of mint sauce spurs the appetite for roast lamb, while doctors have long since proved its efficacy as a major ingredient in stomach remedies; in fact, it is "marvellous wholesome" as an ingredient in digestive medicines today. No longer do we limit its use in cooking to meats; we add mint leaves, dried or fresh, to cheese, fish dishes, fruits, fruit salads, desserts, and sauces; while a few leaves boiled with many kinds of vegetables, or chopped into an oil salad dressing, will improve the tone of any meal. And mint is a great favorite, either as an ingredient or as a decorative, flavorful garnish for desserts and beverages—not only hot or cold Mint tea but also Mint Julep (page 85). As our friend Gerard remarked, "the savor or smell of . . . Mint rejoyceth the heart of man. . . ."

Mint may be grown from seed, but it grows more quickly and you can be more sure of obtaining the species wanted if you buy a plant or beg a root from a friend's garden. Herb specialists and a few seedsmen sell roots by mail. Following are the kinds most useful in cookery. Spearmint, *Mentha spicata,* with long pointed leaves, is easily kept within bounds by cutting tips for use. Curly mint, *Mentha crispa,* is similar but a bit stronger in flavor, and leaves are rounded and curled or crisped. Peppermint, *Mentha piperita,* has a strong flavor, as has its varieties: black mint, *M. p.* var. *vulgaris,* with purple stems and purplish-green leaves, and white mint, *M. p.* var. *officinalis,* with light green leaves, whose aromatic oils are strongest of all in flavor. Apple mint or, as it is often called, woolly mint, *Mentha rotundifolia*, with broad, rounded leaves, has a silvery cast due to the hairiness of the leaves. It is mild-flavored, used in cooking like spearmint. American apple mint, *Mentha gentilis* var. *variegata*, is often said to be the best for indoor growing. Dwarfer than the others, its leaves are grayish-green with light-yellow streaks, and its aroma as well as its taste is distinctly fruity, which leads to its being called at times pineapple mint. Many gardeners maintain it is more immune to insects and diseases than other sorts.

The mints are perhaps the only herbs that in nature grow in light to fairly deep shade and in moist spots. Mint does need light, however, if not sun, and lots of water when grown indoors. Soil should be constantly moist but not waterlogged, and by cutting back the taller shoots and not allowing them to bloom, new low growth will be forced. The pot may soon get full of roots, so that every year or two mint should be repotted —the plant divided, old roots discarded, and only vigorous young roots replanted.

Recipes that include Mint are:

Minted Wine Punch
Strawberry-Mint Wine
   Punch
Orthodox Southern Mint
   Julep
Mint Julep, Yankee Style
Red Kidney-Bean Soup
Yoghurt Beef Soup
Green Bean Soufflé
Mint Sauce Cold
Mint Sauce Hot

Orange and Lemon Mint
   Sauce
Quick Mint Sauce
Minted Sweet Vinegar
Mint Butter Sauce
Applesauce with Mint
Lentil-Soybean Loaf
Greek Salad
Strawberry Delight
Chocolate-Mint Omelet
Apple Pie with Mint

Apple Crisp
Peach Blueberry Cobbler
Apple-Mint Charlotte
Baked Apples
Mint Syrup
Minted Strawberry Tarts
Strawberry-Apple-Mint Pie
Minted Strawberry
   Shortcake
Strawberry Filling

Minted Strawberry
   Meringue Torte
Minted Pineapple Sauce
Hot Citrus-Mint Sauce
Candied Mint Leaves
Bouquets Garnis
Fines Herbes, Blend for
   Vegetables
Herb Vinegar

OREGANO

Origanum vulgare

Also called pot marjoram or wild marjoram, oregano is similar in taste to its close relative marjoram, but its flavor is more pungent and has overtones of mint. The note of mint is hardly surprising since both oregano and mint are members of the Mint Family. The name comes from the Greek: *oros* ("mountain") and *ganos* ("beauty" or "brightness"), signifying that it is not only handsome but also that its habitat was among hills— near the Mediterranean in this case. It is said that oregano originated in Syria and in the upper parts of Palestine. It was well known to the Greeks, and through them, presumably, it found its way to other parts of Europe, with the Romans, as usual, being the agents.

In Greece in olden times it was used not only for flavoring but also for certain medicinal purposes. Many of these remedies carried over into medieval times, with doctors, monks, and old wives perpetuating the tradition. In contemporary cookery the Italians seem to lead the way in using oregano. Indeed, the ubiquitous pizza cannot be contemplated without the thought of oregano as an ingredient. Although Italian cooks may apply it with a more lavish hand than do French chefs, Americans, and others, it is nevertheless a popular herb, often used with lamb, in flavoring grilled chicken, and sauces for certain pasta dishes.

Oregano makes an interesting addition to hearty soups and cold bean salads. It is piquant in marinades for game and game birds and for meats of all kinds; in dressings for green salads and in aspics; in bean or tomato soup; in tomato- and vegetable-juice cocktails; and in stuffings. For poultry, rub the inside with it lightly before roasting, but do not use it if you plan a highly flavored stuffing, particularly one that already has oregano in it. The conflict of flavors or the overwhelming taste of oregano would be fatal. Meats, too, are rubbed with pulverized oregano, as well as the insides of fish, and a few fresh leaves, chopped and added to an omelette, or scrambled eggs, give an extra measure of pleasure. For cooking with flair, boil a few leaves with eggplant, string beans, spinach, peas, onions, or squash, and pour oregano butter over boiled fish just before serving or over shellfish just before baking.

Planting and culture is the same for oregano as for marjoram.

Recipes that include Oregano are:

Tomato Juice Mexicano	*Overstuffed Zucchini*
Herbed Egg Casserole	*Baked Soybeans*
Green Bean Soufflé	*Greek Salad*

PARSLEY

Petroselinum species

What remains to be said about parsley that has not already been known to most cooks? Even beginners find myriad uses for it, while gourmet cooks cannot create their dishes without it. Nonetheless it is not a routine herb. Its taste and flavor contribute to a host of dishes, and as a garnish it imparts a touch of elegance to commonplace foods.

In ancient times the Greeks employed it only for medicinal and ritual purposes—not for cooking; but the Romans made use of it in their cuisine, and their conquering legions took it with them as they moved northward, introducing it into northern Europe and even into Britain. It is reported that they chewed it to rid the breath of garlic and onion odors, since these were staples in their cooking. Sometime later in history its flavorful entrance into all kinds of dishes began and everywhere now people use it as a matter of course.

The many diners who discard parsley garnishes lose more than its piquant flavor. Its valuable nutrients include vitamins A and C and also iron in an easily assimilable form. Thus, dishes to which parsley is added supply nutrients as well as interesting flavor.

Parsley is a biennial, but it is best grown as an annual, for the first year's leaves are superior to the later crops. The flat-leaved type, called Italian parsley, *Petroselinum hortense*, dries more easily and is said to retain its flavor better than curly parsley, *P. crispum*. But curly parsley, with its mosslike, tightly curled leaves, makes a more decorative garnish and seems just as flavorful to many cooks. In fact, I have found the two varieties equal in flavor when dried, although the curly kind requires a longer period for drying.

Indoor growing of parsley is such an old, established custom that it hardly needs description or explanation. Nevertheless there are some considerations often ignored or unknown to the novice herb gardener. Chief among these is the requirement for a deep pot to accommodate the long taproots. Without adequate root room parsley will not produce as well as it should. An 8- to 9-inch pot is adequate and can hold two to four plants. To soften the hard shell and hasten germination, seeds should be soaked overnight in tepid water. It may be sown directly in the pot in which it will grow or started in a seeding medium and transplanted when it has three leaves. Sow twice a year—early spring and late summer—to ensure continuing production of leaves for use, more than one pot may be needed if you have room for them. Parsley has so many uses that there should always be plenty; you can dry or freeze any excess crops.

Recipes that include Parsley are:

Tomato Juice Britannia
Tomato Juice San Fernando
Herbed Tomato Aspic
Herb Dip
Herbed Creamed-Cheese
  Spread
Marinated Mushrooms

French-Fried Parsley
Herbal Broth
Fish Soup à l'Espagnole
Garlic and Egg Soup
Parslied Potato Potage
Tuna-Stuffed Eggs with
  Cucumbers

Ham-Deviled Eggs
Tuna-Deviled Eggs
*Ham Omelette with
  Cucumbers*
Omelette Provençale
Scrambled Eggs with Herbs
Ham-Chicken Soufflé
Seafood Filling (for Crêpes)
Lamb Ragout
Tomato and Meatballs
*Deviled Broiled Chicken
  with Rosemary*
Chicken Cacciatore
Coq au Vin
Chicken à la Marengo
Chicken Fricassee
Herb-Stuffed Roast Rabbit
Rabbit Braised with Herbs
Pesto alla Genovese
Multi-Herb Sauce
Wine Sauce with Shallots
Herbed Curry Sauce
Ravigote Butter Sauce
Parsley Butter Sauce
Green Parsley Sauce

Sauce Rémoulade
*Sauce Verte (Green
  Mayonnaise)*
Sauce Tartare
Rhine-Wine Sauce
*Tomatoes Stuffed with
  Herbed Rice*
Tomato and Corn Casserole
Herb-Stuffed Baked Potatoes
Overstuffed Zucchini
*Green Beans au Jambon
  Julienne*
Lentil Loaf
Lentil-Soybean Loaf
Baked Soybeans
Herbed Soybean Casserole
A Salad of Tossed Greens
*Tomato Salad aux Fines
  Herbes*
Bouquets Garnis
Fines Herbes
*Fines Herbes, Meat and
  Sauce Blend*
Herb Butter
Herb Garlic Butter

ROSEMARY

Rosmarinus officinalis

Romantic legends that entwine with the true history of this woody, shrublike herb are as pervasive as its own pungent fragrance. It has long been a symbol of remembrance—as we know from Shakespeare's Ophelia—and also of constancy and fidelity. Possibly this is why it was woven into bridal wreaths; a bride took a rosemary plant to her new home, and if the plant prospered, she was sure to be dominant. Perhaps some of our militant feminists today should carry a sprig or two as they picket the legislatures.

Among other ancient beliefs was one that rosemary would not grow in the gardens of the wicked. Today it is comforting to know that even though we are not models of rectitude, should rosemary languish in our gardens it is probably due to a *climate* that is evil and wicked. It needs a mild climate, or a cool setting indoors, and it relishes humidity and plenty of water both indoors and outside. It will drop its needles in a hot, dry room or if the soil dries out.

Rosemary comes from the Latin words *ros* ("dew") and *marinus* ("of the sea") in honor of its Mediterranean habitat. Later on, in medieval English, we find this corrupted to *ros-*

maryne, and someone then related it to the Virgin Mary, inventing various confusing but delightful legends to go with this new aspect. In churches it was burned in medieval times as incense to guard against witchcraft and it was also made into charms against the evil eye. Another use was as a strewing herb. It was popularly credited with maintaining youthful looks and spirit if one bathed in a rosemary decoction.

Physicians in old Rome and Greece used it as a remedy for a variety of illnesses, prescribing it for everything from bad breath to loss of hair—it is still an ingredient in hair oils—or from coughs to reptile and animal bites. Some ancient Welsh doctors blandly stated that it was good for *every* bodily disorder, even for relieving headaches and preventing incipient insanity.

For us it is sufficient to know that it makes a good indoor plant (if we are able to meet its needs) that has multiple uses in cooking—on roasts of beef and lamb, broiled veal, on duck and chicken, and in apple-base jelly for serving with pork. Also enlivened by it are baked vegetables and stuffings, while cauliflower, green beans, peas, and potatoes benefit from a bit in the boiling water. Chicken and pea soup as well as minestrone, also marinades for fish—halibut and salmon—gain added zest from a soupçon of rosemary powder.

As you will note from the illustration, rosemary sports fine, needlelike leaves, curved like those of pines, the top a brighter green than the silvery undersides. An erect perennial plant that grows to as much as five feet outdoors, it can be kept to modest proportions of under two feet by pinching back or harvesting tip cuttings, which also make it bushier and fuller. It is slow-growing but needs plenty of pot room. Give it a 10-inch pot whether you grow it from seeds or from started plants you have bought.

Recipes that include Rosemary are:

Strawberry-Mint Wine
   Punch
Fish Soup à l'Espagnole
Tomato Pie Provençale
Ham-Deviled Eggs
Deviled Broiled Chicken
   with Rosemary

Chicken Cacciatore
Dried Black Beans Baked
   with Herbs
Herb Marinade for Beef
   Burgundy and Other
   Meats

SAGE

Salvia officinalis

Wonderfully aromatic, neat, picturesque in habit, sage is a woody perennial of the Mint Family, which one might deduce from its squarish stems. It makes a decorative pot plant, long-lasting and hardy. Although originally a native of warm Mediterranean regions, it has been known to survive outdoor temperatures as low as 15 degrees F. It seems to do best in cool conditions indoors in winter. With daytime temperatures of about 65 degrees maximum and nighttime lows of around 50 degrees, it should flourish rather than merely survive.

Its gray-green leaves, with pebbled, conspicuously veined surfaces and rounded ends, are most handsome. They persist outdoors over the winter, even though affected by frost. Indoors they continue to grow. The normal height of the plant is about two feet, but container-grown plants may be kept as low as a foot tall by cutting back a short section now and then or by pinching out ends of shoots.

Sage is noted for its strong, peppery, rather sharp taste. Therefore it should be used with care lest it dominate rather than enhance the natural flavors of foods. This quality helps it to liven bland foods—cottage cheese for canapés, chicken dishes, poultry stuffings—or serve as contrasting flavor with pork dishes and game, and, as sage butter, give added taste to boiled vegetables.

Its association with pork recipes and goose is traced to ancient times and is of interest not only to the gastronomical historian but also to cooks today. Present-day scientists have demonstrated what old-time cooks knew from experience: sage aids digestion, particularly of fat foods. This is probably why it has been paired for so long with fat fish as well as with pork and goose dishes. A favorite tonic in former times to relieve the doldrums of spring was sage tea, made of dried leaves steeped in boiling water. Even today in rural communities in many parts of the world it is still used for its curative properties. I am witness to the "cosmetic" use of sage, for when I was a boy—at a time when "nice" ladies never dyed their hair—my mother made a strong decoction of sage tea to touch up her few early gray hairs.

Sage can be grown from seed or, if only a plant or two is wanted, you might buy plants from an herb specialist. Cuttings may be rooted, too, and many gardeners make cuttings every third year in order to keep container plants vigorously growing. Because of its unusual leaves sage makes a picturesque pot plant.

Recipes that include Sage are:

*Chicken-Liver Soup with
  Celery
Casserole of Beans au
  Berger
Herb-Stuffed Roast Rabbit
Five-Herb Wine Sauce*

*Baked Soybeans
Herbed Soybean Casserole
Fines Herbes, Blend for
  Vegetables
Fines Herbes, Meat Blend*

TARRAGON

Artemisia dracunculus

Originating in western Asia and the Middle East like so many of our treasured herbs, tarragon became well known long ago in Egypt and Greece. In both countries it was cultivated and developed primarily for its medicinal efficacy; later in history it was called a remedy for "dragon's bite." Presumably it was so used because its dense, serpentlike coiling roots—its Latin descriptive name translates to "little dragon"—made people think it was good medicine for that unlikely malady. As early as the fifth century B.C. its astringent qualities were employed by Greek medics for a number of ailments. Later on it was grown in the royal gardens of Charlemagne. In medieval times it was one of the principal herbs listed in the annals of that great historic Benedictine garden at St. Gall, Switzerland. It was not recorded in England until about Tudor times, when we find it growing again in a king's garden. English doctors treated a variety of illnesses with it.

It was the French, apparently, who discovered its value as a culinary herb. They were the first to employ the admirable *je ne sais quoi* flavor it imparts to vinegar and to certain Dijon mustards. It has a mild anise flavor in its leaves. Possibly the renown of these culinary uses overshadowed its many other uses in cookery, which are less well known but worthy of noting. Many a sauce profits from its tangy flavor—butter sauce for fish, Béarnaise and Tartar sauces, for example—and it has a place in seafood salads as well as in dressings for tossed green salads. Added to tomato soup or chicken broth, it brings a new gusto to these everyday soups. Most seafoods, especially seafood cocktails, are enhanced by its distinctive flavor. A number of vegetables can be' improved by putting a few leaves in their boiling water—spinach, tomatoes, peas, cauliflower, and cabbage. In scrambled eggs and as a flavoring for omelets it is superb. And of course its use in *fines herbes* is legendary. Probably when you grow it you will want to experiment to find new uses for it.

Tarragon may not be the easiest of herbs to grow indoors in containers, but it is well worth the effort. Give it a pot 8 inches in diameter or larger, because it grows rapidly, producing many roots. It may need repotting twice a year. When you divide the roots, replant only a vigorous one, discarding or giving away the others. Be warned: its roots resent excessive wetness; provide good drainage and do not overwater. However, the plant should have adequate moisture for its needs. It will grow about a foot or so high indoors, its very narrow leaves irregularly placed on woody stems. Purchase a plant, for the seed offered does not produce the true French tarragon, since it is usually that of an inferior country-cousin plant.

Recipes that include Tarragon are:

Lentil Soup   *Tuna-Stuffed Eggs with*
Fish or Seafood Mousse   *Cucumbers*

Omelette Provençale
Wine Sauce with Shallots
Ravigote Butter Sauce
Sauce Rémoulade
Sauce Verte (Green
   Mayonnaise)
Sauce Tartare

Tarragon-Mustard
   Mayonnaise
Creamy Cole Slaw Dressing
Tomato Salad
Bouquets Garnis
Fines Herbes, Classic Blend
Herbed Garlic Butter

THYME

Thymus vulgaris

Romantically redolent, the common thyme is a most rewarding herb. Since there are over sixty-odd varieties of thyme, its Latin name should be used in ordering to distinguish it from the other garden varieties. It bears small flowers in June above its small, neat, grayish-green leaves, which grow on persistent woody stems. It is nearly evergreen outdoors in the North, while in mild climates similar to its original native regions of Asia Minor and the Mediterranean it may be evergreen all year outdoors as well as in the house.

In the main in ancient times it was employed in temples where, as in Greece, sprigs were burned as sweet-smelling incense. Later on it was one of the strewing herbs scattered on floors of churches, ecclesiastical buildings, and manor-house banqueting halls. By the twelfth century it had worked its way into cookery, having also many symbolic as well as medical applications. Once called "the emblem of courage," it was cited as a cure for shyness in an early recipe for beer-and-thyme soup.

Because its leaves, though tiny, are strong and pungent, it must be used with caution and subtlety; yet it is an herb that few cooks could dispense with. Tender young leaves, fresh or dried, possess the most of its volatile oils. They should be used to flavor fish, seafoods of all kinds, chowders, vegetable dishes, soups as well as sauces, stuffings, and a variety of meats. Many a meat dish would be poor indeed without its dash of thyme. It stimulates the appetite, aiding in the digestion of fatty foods— which may be one reason that it is a prominent ingredient in sausage recipes. The dried flowers and/or leaves are often combined with rosemary and spearmint to make an aromatic and flavorful tea. This is said to be useful for calming the nerves and for soothing headaches.

Creeping thyme (*Thymus serpyllum*) as well as other flowering thymes that make delightful outdoor plants between paving stones, are of less use for flavoring than the common thyme. Various other thymes with delightful odors are of little or no use in cooking and thus are outside the scope of this book.

Fresh leaves may be used in salads, salad dressings, and for making thyme vinegar. Branchlets may be cut and dried: remove the leaves, discard the stems, and store the leaves for use later on. Thyme is employed in flavoring meats, fish, poultry, soups and chowders, sauces and gravies, in stuffings, and in a variety of egg and cheese dishes. Every three to four years root a cutting or start afresh from seed to keep vigorous plants producing for your indoor garden.

Recipes that include Thyme are:

Marinated Mushrooms   *Casserole of Beans au*
Garlic and Egg Soup   *Berger*
Herbed Egg Casserole   *Chicken Fricassee*
Shirred Eggs with Cheese   *Herb-Stuffed Roast Rabbit*
Seafood Filling (for Crêpes)   *Multi-Herb Sauce*

Herbed Curry Sauce
Five-Herb Wine Sauce
Apple-Horseradish Sauce
Tomato and Corn Casserole
Dried Black Beans Baked
  with Herbs

Bouquets Garnis
Fines Herbes
Herb Vinegars
Herbed Garlic Butter

SOME OTHER HERBS TO TRY

Because the stated purpose of this book is to present those herbs that are most useful in cooking—and the focus is still further narrowed to those that may be successfully and easily grown indoors in containers—many herbs have been automatically eliminated. Some readers may wish to experiment further, once the rudiments of growing plants indoors have been mastered. The foregoing brief lists are by no means the only roster of herbs that may be grown indoors or at least wintered indoors. Many other herbs are possible candidates and have been passed over because they are seldom called for in recipes and hence less worthy of the indoor space required, or they grow too large for the constricted spaces of most houses; others demand such special conditions or extra care that they simply do not belong on an "easy herbs" list.

If you can provide the additional space for more pots and containers, if you can offer the unusual amenities required by some of the plants, and if you can be constant companion and nursemaid to the more difficult ones, then by all means experiment with all those that interest you. To a hobbyist the challenges of indoor growing are part of the joy, with even small successes seeming like major triumphs when the challenges are formidable. Here are a few herbs that offer further territory for adventurous growers to explore. It is not an exhaustive list—there are many others of course—but all of the genera and species, as well as varieties of species, are interesting and all are useful in certain ways.

Garden Cress (*Barbarea vulgaris*) is also called spring mustard or salad cress. It germinates quickly and matures enough in a short period so that it may be cut often, its spicy, pungent flavor adding zest to salads, sandwiches, cream cheese, and other foods. It should be sown at two-week intervals the year round, and may be grown in pots, flats, or even scattered thickly over facial tissues kept constantly moist. Within ten days it is well grown, ready for snipping off and adding to foods. A good variety of seeds is Burpee's 'Curlycress.'

Catnip (*Nepeta cataria*), a perennial herb adored by cats, is reputed to be appreciated by them either fresh or dried. My cats, however, are indifferent to fresh leaves, but in early spring they sport around the plants outdoors as growth begins. Neighborhood cats also pay a call and roll and cavort about the plants. It is easy to germinate seed, or plants may be obtained from herb specialists. Sowing seed in the pot in which it will grow is little trouble. Note that if you have a cat, growing a pot of it indoors may cause trouble if your cat is more susceptible than mine.

Costmary (*Chrysanthemum balsamita*) is also a perennial, propagated by seed or by root divisions, and plants are available from nurseries specializing in herbs. It is floated on beer or ale to add flavor and is also used in flavoring roast beef, hamburger steak, and other meats, in poultry gravy, and in a few other foods.

Lavender (*Lavandula* species) is a pretty, rather woody perennial plant with silvery gray leaves and blue-to-lavender flowers

ABOUT HERBS

that are highly aromatic. Its oils make it useful for antimoth sachets as well as in potpourris. *Lavandula spica* is true lavender, and the other kinds offered by herb specialists and nurserymen are noted mainly for deeper blue flowers or for being fern-leaved or fringed-leaved.

Lemon Balm (*Melissa officinalis*), a perennial, is slow to germinate if propagated by seed, so buying plants is advisable. Add to sauces, soups, stews, egg dishes, salads, and to tarragon vinegar for a different flavor. A leaf or sprig may be placed in long drinks in summer.

Lemon Verbena (*Lippia citriodora*) is aromatic, a perennial that needs to be cut back and repotted each spring. It is useful in flavoring jellies, fruit drinks, and teas, and finely chopped leaves are added to salads. It may be substituted for lemons in sauces and it is also an additive for sachets and potpourris.

Pineapple Sage (*Salvia rutilans*) is a perennial plant with a fruity odor. Chop its leaves fine for adding to fruit salads and to stuffings for game and poultry.

Pot Marigold (*Calendula officinalis*) is not the highly scented annual marigold (*Tagetes* species) grown in our gardens for its flowers but is an annual calendula. Its petals, dried or fresh, may be substituted for saffron. They are added to soups, especially chicken broth, to fish and seafood stews or chowders, and also to pot roasts or braised beef. It may be grown all year, but new plants should be started at least annually.

Winter Savory (*Satureja montana*) is best grown as plants from herb specialists because seeds are slow to germinate. Leaves, fresh or dried, are used in herb mixtures, *bouquets garnis*, many egg dishes, fish, game, meats, and poultry, in sauces and soups,

44

and with green beans. A leaf or two in boiling water with tur-
nips and cabbage cuts down their strong cooking odors. It is
claimed that the gassiness caused by baked beans will be eliminated by adding a few savory leaves before baking.

There are at least two tribes of plants that, although their use
in cooking is minor, make charming indoor plants. There are
two mints in addition to those earlier described:

Corsican Mint (*Mentha requienii*), a tiny-leaved very dwarf
plant, has a strong peppermint odor and taste. It is a miniature
herb, a curiosity and a "conversation piece" plant.

Orange Mint (*Mentha citrata*), also called bergamot mint, has
broad, rounded leaves touched with purple at first, turning later
on to dark green. It is useful for herb teas, and its fresh leaves
added to orange-based summer drinks and punches give a
pleasant taste. Dried leaves keep their flavor very well.

Scented-Leaved Geraniums—more properly called *Pelargoniums*
—offer many flavors and aromas. Placing two or three leaves
in the bottom of a cake pan before adding the batter gives
the entire cake a special fragrance and taste. Apple jelly is trans-
formed from the prosaic into a more rarefied flavor if a leaf is
placed in each glass before the hot jelly is poured in.

These are the more important scents, obtainable as plants
from herb specialists and from nurseries that offer geraniums as
their main stock: Apple, apricot, cinnamon, coconut, eucalyptus,
ginger, lemon, mint, nutmeg, orange, peppermint, pine, rose,
and combinations of some of these scents.

The plants may blossom, but the flowers are generally not
very conspicuous, although they are delicate and dainty, coming
in pink, red, rose, lavender, and whitish. The pelargoniums are

grown for their leaves, not their flowers, and while most require light rubbing to release their leaf scent, a few are aromatic without this. They are also used in sachets and in potpourris.

For further information on growing any of the above herbs, consult herb specialists from whom you buy plants or a good comprehensive herb book that gives full directions concerning soils, water, and other conditions.

II
Planting and Care

3·Techniques of Planting

Methods of sowing seeds or transplanting larger plants or seedlings are quite similar, indoors or outside, except for one aspect:
you are much more in control of conditions indoors. Modern
aids have made the job easy, practically guaranteeing success.
You can govern the temperatures, make sure that proper quantities of water and fertilizers are applied—not too much and not
too little—and correct amounts of light are given for maximum
growth. And because you are dealing with a few plants in containers, not an entire garden, you will have more intimate contact with your plants and enjoy them more.

Older methods that were successful are still good of course,
but busy people who wish to ensure against failure will do well
to take advantage of modern aids and materials. Here are a few
that will lighten your tasks.

Seed-Starting Kits: Several sorts are widely available in garden centers or through mail-order seedsmen. They usually con-
sist of a plastic tray or trays and either a quantity of pellets or
peat pots and a bag of planting mixture to fill them with; often
a small heating cable is included for keeping constant temperatures during germination. All of these individual materials are
also available separately.

Pellets: These are circular, usually about 2 inches in diameter
and compressed to a half inch deep, and are composed of a mixture of peat moss and other moisture-holding materials and

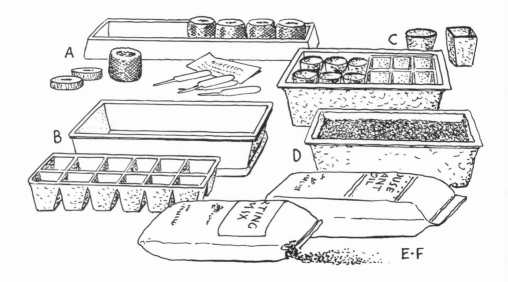

Modern methods of ensuring easy planting and quick seed germination include various planting aids: A. Pellets; when moistened, they expand to many times their dry size. Kits are available, including pellets, a tray to hold moistened, seeded pellets, and marking stakes. B. Pressed peat pots are joined together, fitting into a plastic tray. C. Individual peat pots, square or round, fit into fiber flats. D. Fiber flats are also used for starting seeds in rows or en masse. E. Starting mixtures, used to fill peat pots and flats (B, C, and D) are composed of moisture-holding open-textured materials. F. House plant soil, fertile but sterilized, is used to fill containers for transplanted seedlings.

plant foods. Sold under a variety of trade names (for example, Jiffy-7, One-Step, Bio-gro), some are encased in wide-mesh plastic net, others are completely biodegradable. All when soaked in water expand to about 2 inches high and are ready for planting seeds. As soon as seedlings reach proper size, the entire pellet is transplanted intact into planting soil in the container in which the plant will grow.

Planting Mixtures: Available in bags (or you can make up your own, see p. 60), the mixtures are composed of peat moss, with perlite, vermiculite, or the new Viterra hydrogel—all moisture-holding materials—in balanced quantities. Sometimes stabilizing is achieved by adding sterilized soil. Mixes are useful for filling peat pots or for use in flats when sowing quantities of seeds. For a few plants, such as you will be growing indoors, the pellets or peat pots are easier to deal with than flats.

Peat Pots: Peat moss, plant food, and sometimes a small quantity of wood fiber comprise the materials that are molded under pressure into round or square pots 2¼ or 3 inches across. Filled with the planting mixture (above) and watered, lightly tamped and refilled until mixture is even with the top, they are ready for seeding. (If you start seeds en masse in a flat or pot, you can prick out single seedlings and transplant them into peat pots filled with planting mixture. Grow them on until they are large enough to pot.) When seedlings are ready for final potting, plant peat pot and all, for roots will penetrate the moisture-softened sides and bottom of the peat pot.

PLANTING SEEDS AND TRANSPLANTING

Expand pellets by soaking for five minutes in water to swell them to full size. With a pencil point make a hole in the center of the top. Depth is governed by the size of seeds: large ones should be covered ⅛ to ¼ inch deep, medium ⅛ inch or less. Tiny seeds are sown on the surface.

Sowing: Drop large seeds by hand into the holes or use tweezers to insert them, sowing four seeds per hole. Tiny seeds are more of a problem; crease a 4-inch square of heavy paper across the center. From seed packet carefully shake a small quantity of seeds onto the paper. Hold the paper so that you can incline it to funnel the seeds over the central area of the pellet. A little practice will give you control over distribution. In any case, excess seedlings must be thinned after they are well up, so that only the strongest are retained.

Watering: Pellets. Set on gravel or sand in tray so they will not continue to absorb water but will have sufficient humidity. Never let them get really dry; water lightly and in cloudy weather do not water so frequently. Indoors in dry rooms it may be a good plan to make a little plastic tent over the tray to retain humidity.

Peat pots. There is no way for them to drain, so they must be treated differently. Water them well until the planting mixture is saturated and then sow the seed. Place the pots in a plastic bag and turn the edge over and use paper clips to "seal" it. There

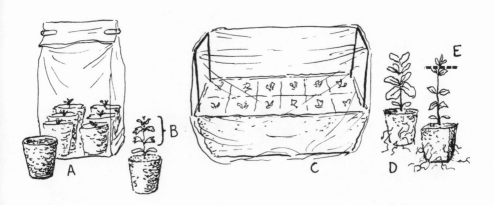

Peat pots filled with moistened starting mixture and sown with seeds are placed in a plastic bag in lots of a half dozen or more. The bag top is turned over (A) and "sealed" with paper clips. Seeds germinate in the pots in room warmth, with no further watering. When they reach the two- or three-leaf stage (B), they are removed, placed in a flat. Bend coat hanger wires to hold a "tent" of sheet plastic (C) tucked under the flat to prevent moisture from evaporating. Keep plants moist, lifting the plastic to care for them, until roots penetrate the side walls of the pots (D). Using thumb and finger nails, pinch out tops of plants (E) to keep them low and bushy.

should be no need for watering until the seeds have germinated. When sprouts are up, remove the pots from the bag and place them on a tray or in a flat. Keep them moist, making a tent of a sheet of plastic as shown in the sketch.

Transplanting: When plants have two or three pairs of true leaves, remove the tent and transplant them to permanent pots,

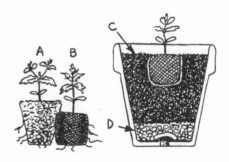

Transplant into final container any time after two or three pairs of true leaves appear. Plants get a better start if roots are well formed, penetrating sides of pots (A) or pellets (B). Make sure containers have good drainage (D). A half inch or more of gravel or coarse material above a piece of broken flower pot covering drain hole will also retain soil. Fill container with moistened soil, press lightly, and set pot or pellet intact in it, the top even with soil. Fill as necessary around it, leaving a half inch or more below the rim to allow for watering. Keep plant well moistened until it is well established.

pellet (or peat pot) and all. Always be sure plants have sufficient moisture, but do not overwater, since only a few thrive in moist situations naturally. See chart p. 61.

Put gravel or other drainage material in the bottom (see illustration), then add with soil mixture and wet it well. (See p. 61 for proper soil mixture according to herb.) Place the peat pot or pellet in the center of the permanent pot, note about how much filling will be needed to bring soil up so that the top of the pellet or pot is a half inch or so below the rim. Lightly firm the soil, then refill until it is the proper height for pellet or peat pot. Fill around the plants with soil, lightly tamping it down with the fingers or a stick, then water, let drain and settle. Refill and repeat until soil is at top of the pellet or peat pot.

Keep the plants out of direct sun for a day or two or until the transplants recover from the shock of transplanting.

Aftercare: To keep plants in good shape, you must repot them from time to time. The time will vary, of course, with the kind of plant. The annuals are best started fresh each year. Some may show signs of continuing, but best growth and harvests come from new plants. The perennials, particularly mints, soon fill the pot with roots and will need repotting every year or two. Also heavy growers, such as tarragon, will need dividing frequently—every year, or less than a year if crowded.

Feeding: Soluble fertilizers are best since you can gauge the amount more accurately. Do not feed newly transplanted seedlings at first. They need time to recover, and food will either be wasted or the plants may suffer from a surfeit. My own feeling is that for regular feedings it is better to use half the amount specified on the label of the fertilizer package than to load the soil with the full amount. Occasionally it will be a good plan to put the pots in the kitchen sink or a bathtub, where they can drain, and "flush" excess salts from the soil by watering and rewatering for a half hour or so, letting the water go through the soil and drain away. This will prevent a buildup of salts, which could cause trouble.

4·Become a Nature Counterfeiter

When we attempt to grow plants indoors in an alien and artificial environment, we must supply as many as possible of the amenities to which Mother Nature has accustomed them over aeons of time. As a good surrogate parent we must therefore counterfeit those conditions with as much understanding and cunning as we can summon, substituting similar situations and offering reasonable facsimiles of the necessary components of soil, moisture, food, and light. We must, of course, learn what the various plants require, for not all plants need the same conditions and treatment, although in general most of our herbs will do quite well with much the same over-all treatment and conditions. Those few that differ in their requirements are covered in the text.

As in many other human endeavors, the picture at first may seem complicated, but experience soon breaks the tasks down into simple routines which knowledge makes rewarding and pleasant.

POTS AND CONTAINERS

Numerous kinds of containers are now employed for growing plants indoors. They range from the conventional clay pot, hard plastic flowerpots, and plastic containers of various sorts and

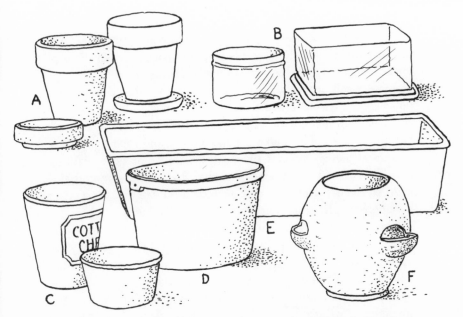

Containers may be anything from clay or plastic flower pots (A) to plastic refrigerator storage containers whose covers often make good water-catching saucers under them. Disposable food containers of plastic (B, C) may be used, well washed, and with drainage holes punched in the bottoms. Paint pots or buckets (D) come in various colors and are good for large plants. Window boxes (E) of any material—wood, metal, or plastic—hold plants in pots or in soil. Pocket planters (F) hold several plants in small space.

shapes (including refrigerator-storage canisters, plastic paint or paste containers from paint stores, and many others) to metal and wooden window boxes. While these all have their merits, they also have certain drawbacks. But all of them usually work pretty well if adequate drainage holes are provided.

Container Qualities: Clay pots and hard plastic pots made for flower growing usually have adequate drainage holes in the bottom. In other receptacles holes must be made. Even herbs that like moist soil do not want it waterlogged. In plastic containers holes are quite easy to make. Hold a large steel nail in pliers over a gas jet until the nail glows red. Then push the nail through the bottom of the pot to make a hole. Reheat and repeat until the bottom is pierced several times—the number of holes varying with the size of the container—so that there will be good drainage. An electric drill with a $\frac{1}{8}$-inch drill bit can also be used to bore holes in plastic as well as in wooden containers.

Clay pots are often preferred because they are somewhat porous and the soil can "breathe" in the pot. However, they are more likely to build up algae and moss, which must be periodically scrubbed off. Many indoor gardeners swear by the hardened plastic flowerpot, and point out that since it does not transpire moisture as do clay pots, less frequent watering is needed. These come in many attractive colors as well as clear, glasslike plastic. Pots of either sort may be set in decorated ceramic outer containers, but you must be sure that bottoms do not sit in water and waterlog the soil. Pots placed on saucers enable you to check the amount of drained water coming out so that you can pour off the excess once the plants have absorbed into the soil all they need.

Window boxes allow for growing a number of plants, provided they all tolerate or demand the same kind of soil and conditions. This simplifies care and has much to recommend it, although a large box, because of its weight, is unwieldy if it must be moved. Some growers put pots in a window box on a bed of gravel and pack peat moss or other material around the pots. This allows the pots to be removed and replaced with ease and simplifies care considerably.

SOIL

The ideal soil for container planting is one that allows water to pass through it. Once this is said it must be qualified. Individual herbs may like a rich or a sandy soil, some like it very open so that little moisture remains, others like it heavy and more retentive of moisture but not to the extent of wetness. In general, however, most herbs are fairly tolerant of soil conditions.

Since only moderate quantities of soil are required for container growing, it is recommended that no risks be taken of introducing disease spores or insect eggs by using nondescript garden soil from outdoors, however good it may seem. It is possible to sterilize such soil by wetting it, then baking it in an oven at 250 degrees F. for forty-five minutes or more, but this is smelly, messy, and time-consuming. Also, given the wide range of soils in our land, the final result is uncertain. It is much better to purchase either the sterilized potting soil—sold even in supermarkets these days—or a soil-substitute mixture, or perhaps to combine both. Jiffy-Mix is a good soil substitute, composed of shredded sphagnum peat moss,* horticultural grade vermiculite,† and certain other elements. Perlite‡ is another additive

---

* Peat moss: Sphagnum peat moss should be used rather than sedge peat, which is quite different. Sphagnum peat moss is sterile, has good moisture-holding qualities, and when shredded will keep soil rather open, yet moisture-retentive.
† Vermiculite: The mineral mica, expanded under heat so that it opens up and "explodes"; helps to aerate soil and yet retains a bit of moisture, as it allows water to drain through. Horticultural grade vermiculite must be specified since builders' grade is coarser and totally unsuitable.
‡ Perlite: Another natural material that is heat-treated, making it light and open. It can be used in place of sand. Where this is not available, birdcage sand (the kind sold for canaries or lovebirds) is a substitute, and it may also contain charcoal and cuttlebone bits, which do no harm and add openness to the soil.

that is useful and completely sterile, moisture-holding, yet allowing drainage.

Using these elements you can make up excellent soil mixtures:

Average Soil Mixture
1 part potting soil
1 part soil substitute

Light Soil Mixture
1 part potting soil
1 part soil substitute
1–2 parts sand or
    perlite

Rich Soil Mixture
1 part potting soil
1 part soil substitute
2–3 parts peat moss

You can also make up your own soil substitute by combining 1 part vermiculite, 1 part perlite, and 1–2 parts shredded peat moss. For plants requiring a somewhat alkaline soil, add pulverized limestone* in the following quantities, level measure, per four cupfuls of mixture: 3–4 tablespoons for average soil, 2–3 tablespoons for light soil, 4–5 tablespoons for rich soil. Mix all ingredients thoroughly. For soils of alkaline-requiring plants, where peat moss has been added in quantity, as in rich soil mixture, the somewhat acid reaction of peat moss should be adjusted by the addition of at least 1 tablespoon limestone. If you use commercial potting soils, they usually have some added fertility, so no plant foods need be added initially.

MOISTURE NEEDS

Too much water may be as bad for plants as too little. Tiny rootlets in waterlogged soil die for want of the air that is as necessary as water for their health. Watering must be governed by the needs of individual plants. (See chart p. 61.) Note, too, that

---

* Limestone: Note that this is pulverized lime*stone*, not the lime used for masonry work, which is deadly for plants. Limestone sweetens the soil, making it less acid and neutralizing it. The pulverized grade may be white or gray, according to the components.

Requirements for Pot Planting

Herb	Soil	Water	Food	Sun	Replant
Basil	A,RI	W,C	M,F	S/PS	Y
Chives	RI	W,G	M,H	S	K-2
Dill	A,RI	W,G	M	S	Y
Marjoram (and Oregano)	A,L	W,C	M,H	S	Y
Mint	B,RI	W,C	M,F	PS/S	K-Y
Parsley	A,RI	W,C	M,H	S/PS	Y
Rosemary	A,L	W,C	M,F	S/PS	RE-4 to 5
Sage	A,L	W,G	M,F	S	RE-3 to 4
Tarragon	A	W,D	M,H	S	K-Y
Thyme	RI,L	W,D	M,H	S	RE-2 to 3

KEY:

SOIL:	A Average	B Humusy	L Light	RI Rich
WATER:	W Weekly	C Moist	G Barely moist	D Dry
FEED:	M Monthly	F Full-strength	H Half-strength	
SUN:	S Full sun		PS Part shade	
REPLANT:	Y Yearly	K Divide	RE Replace, number of years	

NOTE

Weekly watering means soaking pot well. In most cases, if the soil gets dry between, some water should be given, since indoor conditions tend to dry out soil. Where Moist is recommended, never let soil get completely dry between waterings. Feedings recommended refer to house-plant food, diluted according to package directions for full-strength or diluted to half for half-strength. Do not feed during off-season of growth—December and January, and perhaps February for some plants.

the need will vary with the time of year if plants are grown in natural light; and that indoors in winter, in the dry atmosphere, water may need to be added more frequently to compensate for that which is transpired.

City dwellers in areas where water is heavily chlorinated are advised to draw jugs or pans of water the night before its intended use, allowing it to stay uncovered so that the chlorine will evaporate in large measure before plants are watered the following day. Chlorine tends to kill beneficial as well as injurious bacteria in the soil.

Water thoroughly each time, allowing the water to flood the soil until it comes out the drainage holes in the container. Empty excess water from the saucer when plants have fully drained. Or you may immerse the entire pot or container in a bucket of water and allow it to stay until bubbling ceases, then set the pots to drain in a bathtub or sink until the excess is dissipated before returning them to their shelf.

Humidity: A certain amount of humidity in the air is most helpful to plants and is good for humans too. Humidity will retard transpiration of moisture through the leaves into the air and will reduce the need for watering frequently. Even during the winter, when natural light is lowered and days are short, thus slowing growth of plants, humidity is needed. To supply a properly humid environment in the immediate vicinity of the plants, indoor gardeners often use a metal tray about two inches deep and of dimensions to fit the space available. An inch of coarse gravel under the containers permits excess water to drain into the tray when watering is completed, and between waterings a little water added each day will evaporate and keep the air moist.

For growing plants under lights, there are two- to four-shelf models. Lights are set under shelves with deep sides, suited for holding gravel since they are waterproof. (See p. 71.) Further warmth and humidity may be provided for these tiered shelves, or for your own improvised tiers, by hanging large sheets of plastic from the ceiling or a rack to enclose the lighted shelves— a kind of moisture- and heat-retaining tent for the plants. This is a good solution in cool basements or other places where plants may be grown under lights. Heating cables can also be laid on the floor or placed inside the tent to supply warmth. Cables with a built-in thermostat make it convenient and easy to maintain proper heat automatically.

PLANT DIET

Plants may suffer from a surfeit of food if the gardener unwisely overfeeds them. A moderate diet is better, and many experts say that diluting the food to half or a third of what package directions indicate but feeding more often is better for the plants. These are, of course, the commercial plant-food formulas. Natural foods, such as pulverized cow manure, are often advocated, but for indoors they are smelly and slow to release the moderate foods. The same applies to fish emulsion for indoor growing, though it is an excellent fertilizer. If you have pet cats, fish food may prove a road to disaster for your plants.

Commercial fertilizers are adequate, and since we are not growing plants for flowers but for leafage in our indoor herb garden, a high-nitrogen formula would be good to use. The first number in the formula on the package is always nitrogen: 12–6–6 indicates that there is twice as much nitrogen as potash or phosphorus. And for good growth, reasonably well balanced, a 20–20–20 formula is also recommended.

Dilute according to directions, then add enough water to bring the formula down to half or even a third of the stipulated strength. In this way you can supply food every two to three weeks rather than every month to six weeks.

Every six months or less, take the containers to a bathtub or kitchen sink and spray with water to wash dust off the leaves, then water and rewater the soil, flushing out any accumulation of fertilizer salts that may have built up from feedings. The next time you water, after replacing them on their shelf, give your plants the usual amount of food. This regimen should keep all herbs in good trim, growing and producing for you.

SUN OR SHADE

If you are growing herbs in sunny windows, remember that a few need less sun than others. Mint, for example, grows in sun to half shade outdoors, so it can be placed where it gets some shade, or in any case is out of direct sun. Under lights indoors, mint may be placed at the ends of the fluorescent lamps, where light is less intense (it is greatest in the middle section). Or the pots may be placed on the outer edges of the shelf, where they will get plenty of light whose quality is a little less intense than that received directly under the lamps.

Where sunlight is the sole source of light and you have plants needing sun, and space is limited, rotate the plants from time to time—every week or so. Turn your pots around even if you have plenty of space, so that plants do not grow lopsided in reaching toward the light. Where winters are frigid, leaves that come in contact with cold glass are more than likely to be injured. On nights when temperatures fall, cardboard or some other barrier placed between glass and plants will insulate them from the cold.

PESTS AND OTHER TROUBLES

If plants are started from seed, or if purchased plants come from a reputable grower, there is likely to be little chance of pests entering with them. However, in the far from perfect world we live in, where there are other house plants there is always some possibility of trouble entering our Eden.

Because herbs are grown for use either cooked or raw, it would be folly to use the usual chemical pesticides. Only one, Malathion, is relatively harmless and can be advocated for spraying growing plants before you pot them, whether they come from a friend's garden or whether you want to make doubly sure that no insects are introduced with a purchased plant. Spray the plant thoroughly, making sure to hit the undersides of leaves and leaf joints. A few days after you have planted it, wash the plant with a gentle spray, making sure first to cover the pot and soil with a piece of plastic to prevent washing out soil or depositing residue on it.

Should aphids and other pests appear, use an aerosol or other type of spray formulated from rotenone and pyrethrums. These are organic insect killers and are effective except on mealybugs and mites. Mealybugs are small insects surrounded by a white cottony mass, usually infesting the jointure of leaf with stem, but sometimes appearing elsewhere. A cotton swab dipped in rubbing alcohol effectively kills the insect and will aid in removing the mass as well.

Spider mites are visible as rusty reddish sprinklings on undersides of leaves and are not usually prevalent indoors but may come from potted ivy if there are any plants nearby. Malathion will give some control, or a miticide called Dimite may be used according to package directions. Always wash the plants well after a few days and do not use the leaves or sprigs for at least two weeks after that.

Cyclamen mites are too tiny to be seen without magnification, but the effects are visible. Leaves and ends of shoots become twisted, distorted, and curled. Control is obtained by immersing the entire plant and pot in hot water—110 degrees F.—for fifteen to twenty minutes. A gentle spray used afterward will wash off any mites and eggs that have been killed by this treatment. Watch carefully for further troubles, and treat again if necessary.

Mildew is not generally found indoors because of the drier atmosphere. Should it occur, however, washing with a warm soapy water spray is effective in most cases; repeat once or twice if necessary.

5·Let There Be Light

As important in the long run as the kind of soil, fertilizer, or the amount of water you give your herbs will be the light they receive. Without the beneficent sun there would be no chance of green plants existing on this earth. Through a complicated process known as photosynthesis, light enables plants to transform a solution of minerals and foods sent from the roots, into structure—new leaves, stems, twigs, and vital new roots.

Indoors we immediately run into the problem of light—the intensity, the kind, the quality of light that will either slow growth or allow the plant to flourish. Probably you are aware of the pinkish fluorescent lamp introduced some time ago specifically for growing plants and also the cool-white and warm-white fluorescent lights under which many plants will do fairly well. Now there are improvements in the light spectrum, only recently developed, in both fluorescent and incandescent bulbs, which come about as close to simulating actual components of natural sunlight as any we are likely to have for a long time.

These contributions enable us to extend whatever natural sunlight we have for our plants for as long as a summer's day—and for all the year too. By using fluorescent fixtures and by adding a timing device to turn lights on and off (even when you are not home), enough light hours per day can be added to make up the optimum fourteen to sixteen hours necessary to match that ideal summer day. Moreover, timing can be periodically adjusted to lengthen or shorten the supplemental light hours, to compensate as the natural sun wanes or increases its day. Thus electric energy is saved and the cost held to the minimum.

KINDS OF FIXTURES

There are numerous sorts of fixtures for fluorescent lamps, and most are good for certain uses. However, those with reflectors are preferred because all possible energy is directed toward the plants. The more common of these are called industrial fixtures. They may be either permanently secured to a shelf or ceiling or suspended by the chains usually provided with them that allow the fixture to be adjusted up or down. Seedlings and small plants need lights close to them; taller plants should have the lights raised as they grow, as shown in the illustration. These industrial fixtures accommodate two 40-watt fluorescent tubes, the minimum recommended amount of light for growing container plants on a four-foot shelf or table.

There are other fixtures available for less or more space. You should provide 15- to 20-watts light per square foot of shelf space. Reflectorless, or striplights, come in one-, two-, three-, or four-light models in lengths varying from two-foot to eight-foot lengths, the fixtures averaging about four inches longer than the tubes. With these, some means of reflecting light should be improvised in order to lose as little energy as possible. Even painting surfaces above and alongside with flat white is a help.

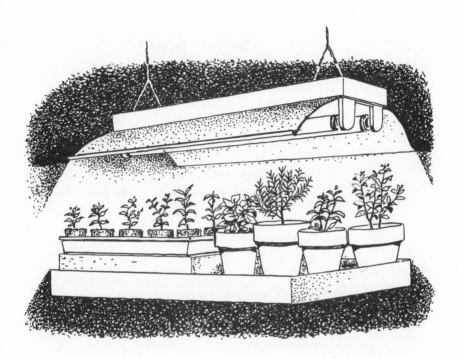

Reflecting fixtures with fluorescent lamps may be adjusted on their chains to the necessary heights above plants. In mixed plantings of tall and small plants, seedlings and low growers are brought up to the proper distance from lights by setting pots on boxes, or blocks of wood. A tray with an inch of gravel in it, on which pots are set, will allow excess water to drain, and also helps maintain necessary humidity.

A FEW GENERAL DON'TS

Do not let wires, and particularly sockets or connections, be placed where they will come in contact with moisture. A short circuit could cause a fire or injure someone. Safety should be your watchword, as it is in using electrical attachments in a bathroom or around a kitchen sink.

Do not leave lights on for a 24-hour day, under the misapprehension that if a 14- to 16-hour day is good, total light would be better. Plants need darkness and rest. Eight to ten hours each day of darkness or near-darkness is necessary for practically all plants.

Do not place lights nearer to plants than the recommended distances or trouble may result. And do not place them at greater distances either; they may not get enough light and, by reaching for it, your plants will be spindly and leggy.

INSTANT-LIGHT SHELVES

A variety of shelves with attached light fixtures or separate fixtures for tabletops are now available. All you need do is to put your plants in place and plug in the electric cord. Several tiered shelves are offered in two-, three-, and four-shelf models. The shelves are made of rust-resistant metals consisting of a one-inch-deep waterproof plant tray above two 40-watt fluorescent lamps in a fixture concealed by the deep sides of the shelf. Each shelf provides about five square feet of plant area, and the shelves may be adjusted on the tubular legs to various heights.

Table models are also height-adjustable and come in lengths of approximately two or four feet, on metal supports. Both these light sources are sold by many garden centers or are available from mail-order seed houses. Timers to turn lights on and off automatically are available in most electrical supply shops.

HERBS UNDER LIGHTS

When you start seeds indoors, lights are a boon. You place your trays of seeding medium, or flats, or pellets (see Chapter III) under the lights and bring the lights to about 5 inches from the top of the seed bed. As seedlings sprout and begin to grow, keep the lights at 5 inches above the tops of the seedlings until they are large enough to transplant into their intermediate pots, or in some cases their final containers, since a few need not be transplanted twice. As plants grow, the lights should be gradually raised an inch or so at a time until at maturity—the level at which you will keep plants cut back—the lights are six inches to a foot above the tops.

There are two manufacturers of fluorescent lamps who feature the newest wide-spectrum light. Agro-Lite,® made by Westinghouse, has a preheating, rapid-start feature and comes in sizes of 18-, 24-, and 48-inch-long tubes. It is recommended that lamps be kept from 6 to 9 inches above plants, perhaps a bit more for mature plants. Duro-Lite Lamps, Inc., manufacture Vita-Lite® and Natur-escent® lights in 24- and 48-inch lengths. Since the Natur-escent® wide spectrum is particularly recommended for foliage plants, it would be the logical choice for herb growing.

INCANDESCENT LIGHTS

In the beginning of limited spectrum fluorescent-light use it was usually recommended that one or two incandescent lamps be installed to add certain rays. Incandescent lights are much more heat-producing than are the fluorescent lamps and cannot be placed as close to plants. However, with the advent of the new wide-spectrum lamps, the range of light rays added by incandescent lights is now no longer needed with fluorescents. And now there is an incandescent lamp that can be used by itself.

Of recent introduction is the incandescent Duro-Lite spotlight called Plant Lite, a bulb with a blue tint in the glass that considerably widens the color-ray spectrum. However, it produces heat and should not be placed closer than 2 to 6 feet. Its use would be limited to a narrow circle of light too, so that on the whole fluorescent lamps would be a better choice.

6·Bringing in the Sheaves

While sheaves may not exactly apply here because we are considering—necessarily—small numbers of container-grown plants, nevertheless it is possible to have more fresh herbs than one needs. If you grow more than a single pot of each kind of herb, you may well be able to harvest and store on a small scale as well as cutting for immediate needs. These "crops" may be either dried or frozen for future use. And as you pinch out, cut back periodically, or do occasional drastic pruning on perennial plants. Rather than discard the cuttings, you may use them if there is sufficient leafage. Keeping plants in shape is more than an aesthetic pursuit—it also keeps them in good growing condition and renewed (in the case of perennials) for continuing production. The time when annual herbs are replaced may also be the time to strip an old plant of foliage before discarding it; then dry or freeze the leaves.

Small quantities of leaves, dried and added to the storage container, build up a fair amount of herbs over a period of time. You may wish to let shoots grow three or four inches longer, rather than pinching out the tips, then cut back and have extra leaves. Keeping plants low and bushy also means that leaves are more closely spaced on the stem. Long, spindly stems are weak and floppy and bear fewer leaves.

There are a few general directions that apply to drying and freezing methods, common to both in the preliminaries:

1. Morning is the best time to cut, because after a night of

rest (even under lights plants have a period of darkness) the aromatic oils are built up, waiting to be released in the daytime. Outdoors it is usually recommended that cuttings be made just before plants bloom. By keeping plants bushy we may prevent them from blooming at all, so we must take leaves and shoots as they get reasonably mature.

2. Thorough washing is needed to remove dust and splashings of soil from the leaves. Do not use hot water—although it is sometimes recommended. Hot water is likely to dissolve those oils mentioned above, robbing the leaves of aroma and flavor. If necessary, use two or more cold-to-tepid waters.

3. Lightly press herbs between two paper towels to blot excess water from the leaves and hasten drying.

4. Pick over the shoots carefully, removing any yellowing or dead leaves, any with spots or blemishes. Remove leaves from the stems unless you are going to hang them to dry or make *bouquets garnis* of them. Most stems become rather woody and do not contribute much flavor.

5. In winter-heated rooms herbs dry more quickly than they would outdoors in the shade in humid summers. Spread the leaves so that they barely touch each other, always in a single layer, on paper toweling or clean wrapping paper. They may be dried anywhere except in direct sunlight. All leaves must be *thoroughly* dry before storage, or mildew may result.

6. A quicker way to dry herbs is to spread the leaves on paper on a cookie sheet and dry them in an oven preheated to 100 degrees F. Do not increase this temperature, and always leave the oven door part way open, about a quarter or a little less. Time needed will vary with the type of leaf, of course; the size, thickness, and structure of the leaves must govern the period. In most cases fifteen minutes will suffice. Check leaves then, and if they are not completely dry and brittle, put them back for a short

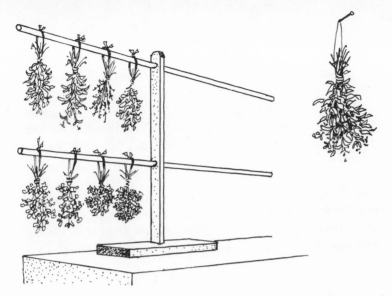

Drying racks allow herbs to be dried in narrow spaces. The vertical member has holes bored in it to admit dowel sticks on which are hung the bunches of herbs. When dismounted, the rack can be stored conveniently and takes up very little space. Tie herbs loosely with tape or string to let air circulate freely through them.

time as needed. Remove from the oven and cool thoroughly before storing.

HERB HANGUPS AND HERB STORAGE

The old-fashioned way of drying was to bunch several sprigs together, tie the herbs with tape or cord, and hang them upside down in a warm attic. If you have an attic, you may still want to do it this way. However, a rack of the sort shown in the illustration will prove adequate even in a small apartment. Check frequently to see how drying is progressing.

Whatever method of drying is used, when sprigs are completely dry, leaves can be crumbled off the stems easily. If you make dried *bouquets garnis,* put them in homemade cheesecloth bags and then store them in paper bags in a cool place until needed. The cloth bags are put into the pan liquid for cooking and are easily retrieved and discarded before the dish is served.

Dried leaves removed from stalks may be shredded, pulverized, or left whole for storage. Air-tight containers are mandatory in order to preserve the full, true flavor. Use dark glass or plastic containers—blue, brown, or green—to retain a more natural color in the leaves. For gifts, decorative clear containers may be used, but for home use there is little point in it, for herbs should be stored in a closed cupboard to retain color and flavor.

HERBS, FROZEN FRESH

Many cooks prefer freezing fresh herbs because the process is quick and the herbs when thawed have a close-to-fresh flavor. Formerly, blanching first in hot water before freezing was advocated, but today we proceed immediately to freezing. Hot water may vitiate the flavor and take away some of the oils. Follow steps 1 through 4 as for drying. Then either make the sprigs into *bouquets garnis* (no cheesecloth bags are necessary) or remove the leaves, chop them or leave them whole, and put them in plastic freezer bags. Heat-seal them and either label each bag as to herb and quantity, if this is pertinent, or put bags in a freezer box and label it if it contains all one kind. As soon as the box is put into the freezer the herbs will begin to freeze. Thaw a bag at a time according to need.

Another method of freezing employs chopped herbs, either one sort or mixtures, measured by spoonfuls, put in ice-cube trays and frozen as soon as water is added. The cubes are stored in the freezer, taken out and used, cube and all. You may wish to use less liquid than is called for in a recipe to compensate for the ice in the cube. A drawback of this method is the amount of space needed. It is not recommended for small freezers or freezer compartments in the conventional refrigerator-freezer.

Packaged frozen herbs should be defrosted at room temperature to retain full flavor. Use immediately and do not refreeze them.

SOME FINAL THOUGHTS

However herbs are stored—dried or frozen—you will have the satisfaction of knowing that they are uniquely your own, since you have grown, harvested, and prepared them for storage when they had reached flavorful maturity.

A few tips may be in order as a guide to preparing and storing certain herbs:

Chives are less flavorful when dried than if frozen, so that they are best used freshly snipped or snipped and frozen. In both cases sort them carefully to remove yellowing leaves and shoots, and keep only plump, green ones. Chop into short pieces —a half inch or less—before freezing.

Dill may also be frozen or it may be used dried. Chop the leaves as for chives when freezing; keep them more or less whole when dried, to help retain flavor.

Savory darkens when dried or frozen, often becoming quite black. This is normal, so do not fret—it loses none of its tang and flavor.

Drying herbs indoors in winter hastens the process because of dry heat, which extracts the moisture more quickly than in spring and summer, when open windows and warm days allow for more humidity. In summer and in humid climates the oven-drying method might be considered.

III
Herb Recipes

7·The Recipes

Since the purpose of growing culinary herbs is to use them, the selection of what will be grown will depend in part on what you like to use them for. Every cook and cook-gardener will probably have strong personal ideas of which herbs are most useful and effective. The recipes presented here are our own selection and may be used only for reference and as a springboard for your own judgment of herb use. Creative cooks will doubtless try other proportions or experiment with other combinations— and that would please us very much.

If you have room for only one or two herbs in containers, and the recipes you wish to use call for others, use the fresh herbs you have and add others bought (preferably) from an herb specialist to be sure of fresh-crop herbs. To substitute a dried for a fresh herb, the usual rule is "use half the quantity of fresh herbs in the recipe." When dry, herb leaves shrink to about half normal size, although retaining most of the flavor. But the rule must be flexible; strength of flavor depends somewhat on the species and varies most with the shelf age of the packaged herb. Moreover, some lose flavor more rapidly than do others: chives have little flavor when dried, while basil, dill, chervil, parsley, and marjoram keep it for upwards of six months. Sage, rosemary, and thyme are good for upwards of a year. Pulverized herbs lose flavor more quickly than whole-leaf or lightly crushed leaves. In any case, smaller quantities of pulverized herbs are needed because the tiny particles pack more flavor per spoonful than coarser bits of herb leaves. Finally, it probably is true that commercially dried herbs lose more flavor than the home-dried ones.

Measure for measure: In a recipe calling for 2 tablespoons of fresh herbs, substitute 1 tablespoon crushed, dried leaves or 2 teaspoons of pulverized herbs. Taste the result; add more if you feel it needs greater flavor. And do not forget to note in your recipe book what you determine is the proper quantity, for future reference.

And if you want to make up your own recipe book, discarding the recipes presented here, dreaming up new uses for them because you disagree with our choices, perhaps the epigram of the late Heywood Broun will be apropos:

"One man's fish is a Frenchman's *poisson.*" (And we presume that the fish will be suitably enhanced with herbs.)

BEVERAGES

Tomato Juice Mexicano

2 cups hearty tomato juice
¼ tsp. onion salt
¼ tsp. dry oregano (or 2 tsps. fresh, finely chopped)

½ cup finely chopped avocado

Put in blender container for 1 to 2 minutes at moderate speed. Serve in a chilled glass over ice cube.
Serves 4 to 5 in juice glasses

Tomato Juice à la Riviera

2 cups hearty tomato juice
3 Tbs. white wine vinegar
12 leaves fresh basil

1 clove garlic, peeled
¼ tsp. salt
1 tsp. lemon juice

Put in blender container for 1 minute at moderate speed. Serve over ice cube.
Serves 4 to 5 in juice glasses

Tomato Juice Britannia

2 cups hearty tomato juice
¼ tsp. salt
½ tsp. Worcestershire sauce

3 sprigs parsley
6 sprigs watercress

Remove large part of parsley stems and woody stems from watercress. Blend for 1 to 2 minutes at medium speed. Serve over ice cube.
Serves 4 to 5 in juice glasses

Tomato Juice Italiano

2 cups hearty tomato juice
2 Tbs. wine vinegar
10 to 12 leaves fresh basil, chopped

2 small onions, diced
½ tsp. black pepper, freshly ground
¼ tsp. salt

Put in blender container for 1 to 2 minutes at moderate speed. Serve in chilled glass over ice cube.
Serves 4 to 5 in juice glasses

Tomato Juice San Fernando

2 cups hearty tomato juice
1 cup diced raw carrot
4 to 5 sprigs parsley, stems
removed

1 Tb. lemon juice
¼ tsp. salt
½ tsp. Worcestershire sauce

Put in blender container for 1 to 2 minutes at moderate speed.
Serve in chilled glass over ice cube.
Serves 4 to 5 in juice glasses

NOTE
Some may like more salt than the amount specified in recipes.
Adjust according to taste.

Minted Wine Punch with Fresh Strawberries

1 pint strawberries
1 cup mint syrup (or honey)
1 pint Puerto Rican light rum
2 bottles (fifths) dry white
wine

1 cup pineapple juice
½ cup lemon juice
2 quarts club soda (or pale
ginger ale)
Sprigs of mint

Pick over, hull, and thinly slice strawberries. Pour mint syrup
over them and refrigerate for 2 hours. Mix rum, wine, pineapple
juice, and lemon juice and refrigerate covered or corked for 2
hours.

Put a block of ice in punch bowl and pour over it the rum-
wine mixture. Just before serving add club soda and strawberries. Serve with small sprig of mint in each punch cup.
Serves about 15 to 20

Strawberry-Mint Wine Punch

2 fifths sweet white wine
  (Sauterne is a good one)
1 quart champagne (or pale
  ginger ale)
4 sprigs mint

1 sprig fresh rosemary
3 pints fresh strawberries
  (or 2 lbs. whole, frozen)
2 Tbs. mint honey
Mint leaves

Cool wine in refrigerator for at least 4 hours. Bruise herbs in bottom of a tall covered crock or jar. Add wine and allow herbs to marinate for 3 to 4 hours at room temperature. Strain out herbs. Crush strawberries, reserving the needed number for use in punch cups when sliced in half. Add honey to strawberries and mix well. Refrigerate for a half hour to 1 hour, then add to chilled wine. Again refrigerate for 3 hours or more. Just before serving, or when you put the wine-strawberry mixture in the punch bowl, add champagne or ginger ale to give sparkle. In each punch glass place a half strawberry and one mint leaf.
Serves 20 to 30

THE MARVELOUS JULEP

Totally American, this drink, of Southern origin, uses bourbon, the American corn whiskey. It has many versions, the Northern variations sometimes nearly touching off a new War Between the States. Not wishing to spark further conflict, I offer the orthodox Southern recipe and one other, which an inventive Yankee worked out. After all, as with any other use of herbs, it *is* a matter of taste, isn't it? And if you like either of them, you might want to plant a few extra pots of mint, just in case.

Orthodox Southern Mint Julep

1 tsp. powdered sugar
XXX
2 tsps. water

2½ oz. bourbon whiskey
Sprigs of mint
Shaved or crushed ice

Dissolve sugar in water in a 12-oz. Tom Collins glass. Fill with shaved ice and pour bourbon over it. Stir, not holding glass, until glass is heavily frosted, adding more ice if necessary. Put several mint sprigs in the glass, letting them protrude 2 or 3 inches, and insert a straw short enough so that it is necessary to bury the nose in the mint when drinking. In this version the mint is for odor, not taste.

ANOTHER VERSION

Pull leaves off 4 sprigs of mint, muddle with sugar in water in the bottom of the glass, then put in whiskey and proceed as above.

Mint Julep Yankee Style

During World War II, I was based in Washington and had a room in a transplanted Massachusetts Yankee's house in Virginia where alcohol was rationed to two bottles a month—a bottle of anything *and* a bottle of whiskey—which meant bourbon. I gave my host my monthly ration of whiskey and was asked by him in return to join the family Sunday afternoons for a julep, served under the mimosa (silk tree) in the backyard. He had his own method of preparing for the julep session, unorthodox according to the Mason-Dixon Line folks, yet interesting to a less prejudiced palate.

He bruised a handful of mint leaves, decanted about a half

cup of bourbon to make space for the leaves in the bottle, and
marinated them for about a week—if he could wait that long.
The nectar was then ready for human consumption—well
minted; even wartime whiskey tasted good to us. About 2½
ounces was poured over crushed ice that filled the glass, a small
sprig of mint was inserted; the Day of the Julep was formally
opened. The reserved whiskey was poured into the bottle with
any that remained and together with the mint already there was
ready for the next session. It was a simple and ingenious way of
saving labor and having instant juleps.

APPETIZERS

Herbed Tomato Aspic

½ oz. (2 envelopes) un-
  flavored gelatine
1 tsp. sugar
2 cans (13½ oz.) tomato
  juice
½ tsp. salt
½ tsp. black pepper,
  freshly ground

1½ tsp. horseradish
  (prepared)
4 Tbs. lemon juice
1 Tb. finely chopped onion
1 Tb. chopped parsley
1 tsp. Worcestershire sauce
1 tsp. celery seed
1 tsp. finely chopped basil
Lettuce leaves

Combine gelatine with sugar in a small saucepan, mixing and
stirring as 2 cups tomato juice are slowly added. Let stand 5
minutes to soften gelatine. Cook over medium heat, stirring
constantly until gelatine is dissolved. Remove from heat and add
the balance of the tomato juice and all other ingredients. Stir
well to mix thoroughly, then pour into custard cups or large

ring or fish-shaped mold. Refrigerate until firm, about 1½ hours. To unmold—run spatula around edge of mold; invert, and shake gently. Turn the aspic out of the mold onto lettuce leaves and serve with mayonnaise in a separate bowl.
Serves 8 to 10

VARIATIONS
Eggs may be added for decorative effect or for extra nutrition. Hard-cook 2 eggs; cool, peel shells, and chop into small dice, adding to mold as aspic is poured in. Or slice eggs and arrange in the ring mold, then pour aspic carefully or spoon it over the eggs until they are well covered, then carefully pour in the rest.

Cooked shrimp may also be added in a similar fashion or served separately, heaped in the center of the ring mold or distributed through the aspic. Marinate 1 lb. cooked shrimp overnight or 8 hours in: 5 Tbs. olive oil, 8 Tbs. lemon juice, 2 cloves garlic, crushed, and 1 tsp. salt. Drain before serving.

Tomato and Herb Spread

2 Tbs. tomato paste or purée
2 Tbs. milk
1 Tb. oil (olive, salad)
1 cup cottage cheese
2 Tbs. chopped walnuts

2 tsps. chopped shallots or
* onion*
2 tsps. finely chopped basil
2 tsps. finely chopped chives
2 tsps. lemon juice
Parsley, for garnish

Mix tomato paste with milk to smooth, adding oil gradually until mixture is smooth and quite liquid. Put cottage cheese in a bowl and add paste mixture, mix lightly, then add all other ingredients and mix. Serve in a bowl with sprigs of parsley decorating the rim or placed around the bowl on the plate.
Yield: about 1½ cups

Herb Dip

1 cup tarragon mayonnaise*
½ cup dairy sour cream
1 Tb. grated onion
1 tsp. finely chopped chives
1 tsp. chopped parsley
¼ cup grated raw carrot

1 Tb. grated raw radish
Salt to taste
Black pepper to taste, freshly
ground
Paprika

Combine sour cream with mayonnaise, then stir in balance of ingredients. Refrigerate until ready for use. Sprinkle dip with paprika after it is put into bowl. Serve with chips, thin-sliced pumpernickel squares, or crackers.
Yield: about 1¾ cups

---

* Mayonnaise made with tarragon vinegar.

Herbed Creamed-Cheese Spread

1 shallot, finely chopped
1 heaping Tb. each:
    chopped chives
    chopped parsley
    chopped chervil*
1 cup pot cheese*
¼ tsp. salt

⅛ tsp. black pepper, freshly
ground
3 Tbs. wine vinegar
4 Tbs. oil
1 cup heavy cream,
whipped

Mix the chopped shallot and herbs in a bowl with the cheese, then add oil and vinegar. Mix well, then fold in whipped cream

---

* **Substitutions:** If fresh chervil is not available, add equivalent amount of parsley. Cottage cheese, the tiny-curd type, may be used in place of pot cheese. If creamed, it may make the mixture looser and will require draining longer. Or it may be served undrained in a bowl as a dip.

and seasonings. Line a large strainer with cheesecloth and put the mixture into this to drain in a cool spot. Allow to drain for 4 hours, then turn out on a plate, remove cheesecloth, and serve with thinly sliced rye bread or pumpernickel.
Yield: about 1½ cups

Marinated Mushrooms

1 lb. button mushrooms
½ cup water
½ tsp. salt
Juice of ½ lemon
½ cup red wine vinegar
8 Tbs. olive oil
1 bay leaf (optional)

2 small cloves garlic,
  crushed
¼ tsp. thyme
½ tsp. coarsely ground black
  pepper
2 Tbs. finely chopped
  parsley

Wash mushrooms well, trimming off stems. Place in a pan with cold water and salt and bring to boil over low to medium heat. Lower heat and simmer 10 to 15 minutes. Drain, and put mushrooms in a wide, low bowl.

Combine all other ingredients except parsley in an enameled or stainless-steel pan and bring to the boil, lower heat, simmer for 15 to 20 minutes. Pour hot mixture over mushrooms, cool, and let marinate in refrigerator overnight or longer. Drain, arrange caps on serving plate with toothpicks nearby, sprinkle parsley over the tops.
Serves 6 or more

NOTE
Reserve stems of mushrooms after draining marinade and use next day in an omelet, or use before marinating.

French-Fried Parsley

Several years ago at a dinner the guests were mystified when a plate of something crisp, dark green, and aromatic was passed. It proved to be curly parsley, deep-fat fried. Not only was it a splendid conversation piece, it was even more appealing as a tasty garnish. Curly parsley is best, but any parsley will do. Italian parsley may be a little fragile, but if handled carefully will hold together.

2 (or more) sprigs parsley   *Oil for deep frying*
  per person

Heat oil in a deep pan to 360° F. Using tongs to hold stems, immerse parsley in hot oil for 1 to 2 minutes. It should be somewhat crisp when removed. Drain on paper towel, put on a pie tin, and place in a heated oven for 2 or 3 minutes. (When serving with roasted meat, put in oven as roast is removed.) Carefully arrange on a serving plate that has been warmed. Most guests will eat it holding the stems in their fingers.

A SALUTE TO SOUP

A fixture through the centuries in every cuisine of the world, soups range from delicate and elegant to the robust, hearty peasant fare that enabled the plain people of the world to survive calamity and catastrophe. Perhaps because soups are so familiar to us they are often taken for granted, even scorned by some self-styled gourmet cooks. Yet soup can make a whole meal by itself, and a remarkable one, with only the addition of a bit of bread, a green salad, and perhaps some wine and cheese as a dividend to the delicious mainstay of the meal. Or a good soup can give a dinner the send-off that sets the tone for the rest of the menu.

Herbs are often the key ingredient in a soup, giving it an indefinable aroma and taste that lifts soup from the category of mere food and transports it into a more exalted realm. Herbs are a godsend, too, when unexpected guests drop in and must be invited to stay for luncheon or when Sunday-dinner invitees enjoy your company so much that they linger and must be given a light supper before being sent on their homeward trek. Soup is the answer—a can or two from the storage shelf, a bit of hand-is-quicker-than-the-eye magic with herbs, and *presto!* the memorable soup the results of which might linger longer in the memory of the guest than the special recipe you slaved over for a full day as the main course of dinner.

Soups are capable of infinite variations. You can be as creative as you wish with them, experimenting with various herbs and noting the results, gradually building a repertoire of soups that are made your very own by the way you use your home-grown herbs.

A good hot soup will cheer the spirit on a gray day when blustery bone-chilling winds take the joy out of life. Cold soups make the dog days of summer more bearable and herbs help to enhance the cooling effect. Herbs, therefore, have a role to play in making hot or cold soups individual, most pleasurable experiences for your family and your guests.

Lentil Soup

1½ cups lentils
  3 pints stock (or bouillon,
    diluted)
½ tsp. salt
  3 Tbs. olive or salad oil
2 carrots, diced
1 Tb. celery seeds, mashed
  (optional)

1 large onion, chopped
1½ cups tomatoes, canned
  or fresh, chopped
2 stalks celery and tops,
  chopped
½ tsp. grated lemon rind
1 tsp. lemon juice
½ tsp. dried tarragon

Wash lentils and put in large pot, add stock and salt. Cover and simmer over low heat until lentils are almost tender, about 1 hour. Add all other ingredients and cover. Simmer until carrots are done, about 15 to 20 minutes longer.
Serves 6

Red Kidney-Bean Soup

2 cans (15½ oz.) red
  kidney beans
1 or 2 cloves garlic, minced
2 medium-sized onions,
  chopped
2 oz. unsalted butter
1 Tb. dried mint leaves (or
  3 Tbs. fresh, chopped)

2½ cups beef bouillon
  3 Tbs. oil
  1 cup yoghurt
½ tsp. salt
Several sprigs fresh mint
Slices of lemon

Put beans in blender container and blend at medium speed until puréed. Melt butter and sauté onion and garlic until golden. Put mint leaves, beef bouillon, oil, yoghurt, and salt in blender with bean purée and blend at medium-high speed until

well mixed, about 1 minute. Put in a pan with onion and garlic and heat thoroughly. Serve with a sprig of fresh mint in each soup dish and lemon slices on the side. A dish of yoghurt may also be passed, if desired, to be spooned on top of hot soup. Dark rye bread or pumpernickel goes well with it.
Serves 5 or 6

Herbal Broth

2 Tbs. butter, melted
3 Tbs. flour
5 cups chicken stock (or canned chicken broth, diluted)

2½ Tbs. mixed fresh herbs (basil, chives, parsley) chopped
1 small clove garlic, finely chopped
3 to 4 Tbs. cream

Melt butter in pan and sauté flour in it, adding herbs when flour is lightly browned. Sauté herbs 1 minute. Add slowly 1 cup of heated stock, stirring to smooth, then add to stock over low heat and cook 20 minutes. Cream can be added shortly before taking from heat and stirred in.

This broth can be made ahead, refrigerated, and reheated before serving. It also can be the basis for other soups, for instance, Herbed Chicken Giblet Soup, below.
Serves 6 to 8

Herbed Chicken Giblet Soup

3 eggs
2 Tbs. butter, melted
1 small clove garlic, minced

1 medium onion, chopped
1 small stalk celery, chopped

Flour
¼ lb. chicken hearts,
   chopped
¼ lb. chicken gizzards,
   chopped

1 Tb. flour
5 cups Herbal Broth (see
   above)
1 Tb. butter
Salt and pepper to taste
¼ lb. chicken livers

Hardboil eggs and cool. Sauté celery with onion and garlic in butter until onions are golden. Sprinkle hearts and gizzards with flour, add, and cook 3 to 4 minutes. Put all in a pan of Herbal Broth and simmer until tender, about 1½ hours. Rub chicken livers through a sieve and mix with 1 tablespoon flour and 1 tablespoon butter. About 10 minutes before soup should be done, add to broth mixture and turn down heat a little. Coarsely chop eggs, and just before serving, stir in, adding salt and pepper to taste.
Serves 6 to 8

Fish Soup à l'Espagnole

Adapted from a Spanish recipe

3 lbs. lean white fish
2½ quarts (10 cups) water
⅓ cup olive oil
1 medium onion, finely
   chopped
1 medium tomato, chopped
   (or ½ cup canned, with
   juice)
4 thick slices whole wheat
   bread, cubed

12 to 14 blanched almonds
4 small cloves garlic, peeled
1 Tb. chopped parsley
½ tsp. rosemary, pulverized
Juice 1 lemon
½ cup fresh orange juice
Salt and pepper to taste

Cut fish into slices 2 to 3 inches wide and salt lightly. Refrigerate

1½ hours. Boil fish in 2½ quarts water for 15 to 20 minutes. Heat olive oil and fry onion until deep golden, add tomato and cook for 3 to 4 minutes. Add onion-tomato-oil mixture to fish and keep at low boil for 15 minutes more. Put bread cubes in the bottom of another pot and strain fish mixture over it. Reserve fish. Return soup to heat. Crush herbs, almonds and garlic together (or put in blender) and add to soup. Simmer while removing skin and bones from fish. Add fish flesh to soup and stir well. Add lemon and orange juice, season to taste, and reheat. Serve hot with slices of garlic bread.
Serves 6

Garlic and Egg Soup

Adapted from a Spanish recipe

1 bulb garlic
3 Tbs. olive oil
8 cups water
6 sprigs parsley (or 4 tsps. dried)
Small bay leaf
¼ tsp. pulverized sage
¼ tsp. pulverized thyme

4 cloves (spice)
1 to 2 tsps. salt
White pepper, to taste
French bread, sliced, toasted
½ cup grated Parmesan cheese
6 to 8 eggs (to poach)

Separate garlic into cloves. Put in boiling water for 1 to 2 minutes, remove and drain; peel. Add cloves to 8 cups water and all other ingredients except bread, cheese, eggs. Boil gently just above a simmer for ½ hour or a little longer. Taste, add more salt if desired. Strain and discard all herbs, return to pot and simmer for 15 to 20 minutes longer. Meanwhile poach eggs separately but just slightly underdone. Ladle soup into bowls, put a slice of toasted bread in each and a poached egg

on top of toast. Pass cheese to sprinkle over egg and toast.
Serves 6 to 8

VARIATIONS

1. Break eggs carefully, salt them to taste, and slide onto
surface of simmering soup to poach. Ladle out and serve in
bowl, pouring soup over them. Serve toasted bread separately.

2. Put slices of toast in cooking soup and break them up
with a spoon. Pour out soup into a flat earthenware casserole.
Beat eggs with a little salt until lightly frothy; spoon on top
of soup and bake uncovered at 300°F. for a few minutes to form
an egg crust on top of the soup. Or stir beaten eggs into the
simmering soup, cook for 5 minutes, and serve over toast slices.

BLENDER SOUPS

Yoghurt Beef Soup

*Said to have originated in the Near East or Turkey. I find the
story unlikely because of the beef content. However, the soup
itself needs no apology and should answer any questions.*

3 pints beef stock	2 Tbs. soy flour
3 Tbs. wheat germ	1/4 cup whole wheat or rye
1/2 tsp. salt	flour
1/4 tsp. black pepper, freshly	3 Tbs. olive oil
ground	2 cups yoghurt
1/4 cup fresh mint leaves (or	
1 Tb. dried)	

Put 1 pint of stock in blender, add all other ingredients except
yoghurt. Blend for 2 to 3 minutes at medium speed, then add
balance of stock and yoghurt and blend for 2 minutes, or until

smoothly blended. Heat thoroughly before serving.
Serves 6

Soupe au Pistou

*Some call it a simplified version of minestrone, and possibly it
is, since it comes from southern France near the Italian border.
It may be served hot in winter or cool—not chilled—in summer.
Fresh vegetables as listed here or others substituted according
to availability may be used, but always include ripe tomatoes.*

2 Tbs. olive oil	*3 carrots, scraped, diced*
1 large onion, thinly sliced	*3 medium potatoes, peeled,*
1 cup shelled fresh baby	*diced*
limas	*Water*
½ cup Frenched green beans	*Salt to taste*
3 small zucchini, sliced	*Pepper to taste*
3 firm tomatoes, peeled,	*½ cup vermicelli*
chopped	

Pistou*:

3 cloves garlic	*¼ cup grated Gruyère*
⅔ cup fresh basil leaves or	*cheese†*
⅓ cup dried basil	*5 Tbs. olive oil*
¼ tsp. salt	*Extra grated Gruyère cheese†*

In a large pot cook onion in the olive oil until deep golden,
then add vegetables with enough water to cover them, about
2 inches deep. Bring to a boil, reduce heat, add salt and pepper,
and simmer covered for about 45 minutes or until potatoes
and carrots are tender. Add vermicelli and simmer for about
15 minutes longer.

Meantime make the *pistou* (or it can be made earlier) by pounding in a mortar all ingredients except olive oil, then add oil a drop or two at a time. It can also be made in a blender, again adding oil slowly.

Serve hot, adding the *pistou* to the reheated soup just before serving. To serve cold, add just before serving and mix well. In both cases pass a bowl of grated Gruyère cheese to sprinkle on top of the soup.

---

* **Substitution:** Instead of this **pistou,** Pesto alla Genovese, p. 130, may be used.
† Grated Parmesan cheese may be substituted for Gruyère.

Chicken-Liver Soup with Celery

½ lb. chicken livers, broiled
   or sautéed
1 small onion, coarsely
   chopped
2 Tbs. butter
¼ cup celery and tops,
   chopped

¼ cup olive oil
1 quart milk
1 tsp. salt
3 Tbs. whole wheat or rye
   flour
3 Tbs. soy flour
¼ tsp. dried, pulverized sage

If sautéing livers, melt butter and sauté onion first, then add livers and sauté over medium heat for 3 or 4 minutes. They should be cooked through, but tender, not hard. Put celery and oil in blender and blend at high speed for 1 minute, then add milk, salt, flour, and sage, and blend at medium speed 1 minute before adding onions and liver. Blend until smooth, heat thoroughly, and serve. Garnish with half slices of lemon if desired.
Serves 6

COLD SOUPS

Parslied Potato Potage

While this may not be memorable enough for anyone to sell his birthright for a "mess of potage," so to speak, it is a wonderfully cooling soup to start a summer luncheon with.

2 large boiled potatoes
1 Tb. butter
4 medium onions, finely
   chopped
3 cups milk
2 Tbs. finely chopped chives
⅛ tsp. black pepper, freshly
   ground

Salt to taste
  8 to 10 sprigs French-fried
    parsley (p. 91)
  1 cup yoghurt (½ pint)
  ¼ cup parsley, finely
    chopped

Potatoes should be soft enough to be sieved.* Put through sieve. At least 1 cup or more of sieved potatoes is needed. Melt butter and fry onions until lightly browned. In top of double boiler over boiling water heat milk, but do not let boil. Add sieved potatoes gradually, stirring to mix well. Add onions, chives, seasonings, and French-fried parsley, well chopped. Simmer over moderate heat then remove and cool. Refrigerate. When ready to serve, add yoghurt, about a third at a time, stirring well. Soup should not be thin, but about consistency of heavy cream. Garnish each serving with chopped fresh parsley. Serves 4 to 5

---

* Mashed potatoes may be substituted but should be sieved to make certain lumps are removed. Potatoes should be freshly cooked.

Cucumber and Yoghurt Soup

3 cups yoghurt
2 Tbs. olive oil
1 tsp. lemon juice (or grated
  lemon rind)
1 clove garlic, minced
1 cup consommé, chilled
1 tsp. dill seed (optional)
2 Tbs. chopped chives

½ tsp. salt
¼ tsp. black pepper, freshly
  ground
1 cup diced, peeled
  cucumber
2 Tbs. finely chopped chives
  (for garnish)

Put all ingredients except cucumber in blender container and blend at medium speed for 1 or 2 minutes. If dill seed is used, mash lightly before putting in blender. If a thick soup with a cucumber flavor is desired, add cucumber and blend for 1 minute. Or add first mixture to diced cucumber and refrigerate in a bowl until well chilled. Garnish soup with chopped chives. Serves 4 to 6

AN UNUSUAL TOMATO PIE

Tomato Pie Provençale

9-INCH PIE CRUST, BAKED
4 Tbs. olive oil
6 large ripe tomatoes
2 Tbs. tomato purée
3 Spanish onions
½ tsp. salt

2 Tbs. butter (sweet)
½ tsp. rosemary, well
  chopped
2 Tbs. Parmesan cheese
Small can anchovy fillets
Black olives

Heat oil in pan, add tomatoes (chopped, skinned, and seeded), salt, and tomato purée. Cook over low heat until excess moisture has evaporated, mashing as you stir to blend all tomatoes into purée. Slice and simmer onions in butter, adding rosemary after 1 minute, until onions are golden. Sprinkle bottom of pastry with cheese, add onions, then cover with tomato purée mixture. Drain anchovies and arrange in lattice pattern over top. Slice ends off black olives and place one round in each lattice square. Brush olives and anchovies with a little oil, then bake quickly in preheated oven at 350°F. for 10 minutes. Reduce heat to 300° and bake for 20 to 25 minutes longer, or until filling is set. Serve hot.

Serves 6 to 8

PASTRY FOR TOMATO PIE

1 cup sifted flour	*1 Tb. vegetable shortening*
¼ tsp. salt	*3 Tbs. very cold water*
5 Tbs. sweet butter	

Sift flour and salt into a mixing bowl, add butter and shortening and cut into flour with a pastry cutter until mixture resembles fine bread crumbs. Add cold water and work in lightly with a fork. Make a ball of dough, wrap in foil or plastic and chill in refrigerator at least 3 hours; overnight is better. Roll out dough on floured pastry board until circle is large enough to fit 9-inch pan. Line pan with dough, crimping edges, and place an 8-inch pan on top—or weight with rice or dry beans—to prevent crust from puffing and humping when baked.

Bake in preheated 400°F. oven for 5 minutes, lower heat to 350°. Bake about 10 minutes longer or until light golden brown. Do not overbake. Remove from oven and cool before filling with tomato mixture.

Makes 1 crust for 9-inch pan

EGG DISHES

Herbed Egg Casserole

12 hard-cooked eggs
1 small clove garlic
1 tsp. dried thyme
2 tsps. dried basil
4 tsps. mayonnaise
1 tsp. herb vinegar
2 tsps. dried oregano (or

3 tsps. marjoram)
1/4 tsp. salt, or to taste
1/8 tsp. black pepper, freshly
   ground
1/2 tsp. curry powder
1 pint sour cream
Paprika

Cut eggs in half, remove yolks. Press garlic and discard pulp, mix juice with egg yolks; add all other ingredients except curry powder and sour cream. (If dried herbs are not finely broken, pulverize in a mortar, so that no lumps of herb remain.) Fill centers of egg whites with this mixture, heaping it up a little. Mix curry powder with cream.

In a large shallow baking dish (or in two casseroles) arrange the filled egg halves in one layer and pour sour cream over them. Bake uncovered in a preheated 375°F. oven for 15 to 20 minutes or until cream is somewhat thickened. If desired, as soon as dish is removed from the oven, sprinkle paprika over the top. This adds to flavor and appearance of dish, but too much may overbalance delicacy of the dish. The highly seasoned eggs should always dominate the taste.

Serves 6

Eggs with Tomatoes and Cucumbers

8 hard-cooked eggs
1 medium cucumber
½ cup French Dressing
  (p. 159)
4 green olives, pitted,
  sliced

Ripe olives, pitted
  (optional)
1½ cups Green Mayonnaise
  (p. 140)
Parsley sprigs for garnish
6 to 8 ripe tomatoes

Shell eggs and slice evenly. Do not peel cucumber but score`
lengthwise with a fork, then slice moderately thin. Slice tomatoes
thin, seed and drain. Place cucumber in a bowl and then pour
over the French Dressing. Mix well, then remove cucumbers
and put tomatoes in dressing. On a large plate or platter arrange
alternate groups of 2 or 3 slices of tomato and 4 to 6 slices
cucumber around outside edge. Ripe olives may be placed
evenly among them. Put a bowl containing the mayonnaise in
the center and arrange sliced eggs around it, or arrange eggs
and spoon mayonnaise into a mound in the center. Garnish with
parsley.
Serves 4 to 6

Tuna-Stuffed Eggs with Cucumbers

8 hard-cooked eggs
4 Tbs. shredded tuna fish
4 Tbs. mayonnaise
1 tsp. finely chopped tarragon
Salt and pepper (optional)
2 Tbs. parsley, finely chopped

1 Tb. finely chopped chives
1 Tb. lemon juice
1 small cucumber
1 cup Red Mayonnaise
  (p. 139) or Green Mayonnaise (p. 140)

Shell eggs and cut in half lengthwise. Scoop out yolks and mash them with tuna fish and 4 tablespoons mayonnaise, season if necessary, then mix in chopped herbs with lemon juice. Peel and slice cucumber, soak in cold water with 1 teaspoon salt 20 to 30 minutes, drain and pat dry. Fill whites of eggs with tuna mixture, mounding it up ball-like over the cavity to make an egg shape, half egg, half tuna. Serve on lettuce leaves, with eggs and cucumber slices arranged around a bowl of mayonnaise, either red or green.
Serves 4 to 6

Ham-Deviled Eggs

12 hard-cooked eggs
5 to 6 Tbs. cooked ham,
    very finely chopped or
    twice ground*
½ cup mayonnaise
¼ tsp. pulverized rosemary

1 Tb. Dijon mustard
½ tsp. salt
¼ tsp. powdered onion
1 tsp. red wine vinegar
2 Tbs. finely chopped
    parsley or chives

Cut eggs in half lengthwise, remove yolks and reserve whites. Mash yolks with a fork; add other ingredients except parsley or chives and mix well until smooth and well blended. Fill each yolk cavity in whites with mixture, mounding it well. Garnish with parsley or chives.
Serves 12

---

* Canned deviled ham may be substituted, but use half quantity of rosemary and onion powder.

Tuna-Deviled Eggs

12 hard-cooked eggs
4 Tbs. mayonnaise*
1 Tb. herb vinegar
½ tsp. salt
¼ tsp. white pepper
5 Tbs. tuna fish, shredded

¾ tsp. dry mustard
1 tsp. Worcestershire sauce
   (optional)
Paprika
Sprigs of parsley

Cut eggs in half lengthwise, remove yolks and reserve whites. Mash yolks with a fork; add other ingredients except paprika and parsley and mix until completely blended. Fill each yolk cavity in whites with mixture, mounding it up well. Sprinkle with paprika and garnish with sprig of parsley.
Serves 12

---

* Green or Red Mayonnaise (pp. 139, 140) may be used, in which case use plain, white vinegar.

Omelette Provençale

8 eggs
2 Tbs. butter
2 Tbs. water
Salt and pepper to taste
2 small onions, finely
   chopped
2 cloves garlic, peeled, finely
   chopped

4 medium tomatoes
4 sprigs fresh tarragon,
   finely chopped*
½ cup fresh parsley, finely
   chopped
Salt and pepper to taste
4 Tbs. butter or olive oil

Break eggs and season; set aside. Combine onions, garlic, tomatoes (peeled, seeded, and chopped), herbs, salt and pepper.

Sauté in oil or butter for 10 minutes, stirring in the pan. When cooked, keep warm.

Beat eggs lightly with 2 tablespoons water and cook quickly in the butter, lifting edges with a fork or spatula to allow eggs to run under cooked portion. When cooked but still soft, spread vegetables on top and fold the omelette over. Serve at once on a heated dish.

Serves 4 to 6

NOTE
For most satisfactory results, divide the recipe in half, cooking 4 eggs at a time and making two omelettes.

---

* Basil may be substituted for tarragon.

Ham Omelette with Cucumbers

4 Tbs. diced cooked ham	*1 tsp. finely chopped chives*
3 Tbs. diced cucumber	*1 tsp. parsley*
4 to 6 eggs	*⅛ tsp. pulverized sage*
Salt and pepper to taste	*2 Tbs. butter*

Cut leftover or other boiled ham into ¼-inch dice. Peel and dice cucumber and immerse in boiling water for 2 minutes. Drain and blot dry. Beat eggs well and season; reserve. Sauté ham, cucumber, and herbs in melted butter for about 5 minutes, stirring constantly; when done, set aside and keep warm. Make omelette in usual fashion, and when done but eggs are still soft, spoon ham-cucumber mixture on and fold omelette over. Serve immediately on a warmed plate.

Serves 3 to 5

Scrambled Eggs with Herbs

3 Tbs. butter   ½ tsp. salt
8 eggs   ⅛ tsp. white pepper
3 Tbs. finely chopped parsley   4 Tbs. light cream

Melt butter in frying pan over low heat. Break eggs into skillet, or into a bowl, and stir vigorously, adding seasonings and cream. Mix well. As eggs begin to cook and set, lift with a spatula and let uncooked liquid flow under to cook. Eggs are done and should be served when they are well cooked but still shiny and moist.
Serves 4 to 5

VARIATIONS

With cheese: grated Gruyère or Parmesan cheese may be added, 2 to 4 tablespoons, according to taste. Also, natural Swiss cheese may be cubed and added, about ⅓ cupful for above quantity. Substitute ⅛ teaspoon powdered sage for parsley.

With shrimp: Wash and pick over ¼ lb. baby shrimp and lightly sauté in 1 tablespoon butter and pressed juice of 1 clove garlic. When warmed through, add to eggs in pan and stir in well. Substitute ⅛ teaspoon pulverized thyme for parsley.

With bacon: Fry 4 slices lean bacon until well crisped, drain on paper towel. Chop bacon until all pieces are small and combine with 2 tablespoons finely chopped parsley and 2 teaspoons finely chopped chives. Add to eggs.

With ham: Dice ham in ¼-inch pieces to make ⅓ cup. Add to eggs when almost set. Garnish with chopped parsley when serving, or add parsley with ham. Also, a combination of ham and cheese may be added, with chopped chives used for garnishing.

With mushrooms: Wash fresh mushrooms (about 6 oz.) and cut in ¼-inch slices, stems and all. Sauté in 2 tablespoons butter until golden. Cook eggs until almost set, stir in cooked mushrooms. Serve, sprinkled with 2 tablespoons finely chopped parsley.

Shirred Eggs with Cheese

Butter
6 Tbs. fresh bread crumbs
¼ tsp. pulverized dried thyme (or 2 tsps. finely chopped fresh basil)
12 thin slices imported Swiss cheese
6 slices from large tomato
Dash pulverized thyme (or 2 tsps. finely chopped fresh basil)

12 Tbs. heavy cream
6 large eggs
¼ tsp. salt
⅛ tsp. black pepper, freshly ground
Paprika
2 Tbs. grated Gruyère cheese

Butter well the sides and bottoms of 6 ramekins.

Melt 1 tablespoon butter in a skillet over low heat and add thyme (or basil) and mix. Add bread crumbs and stir, allowing them to absorb butter.

Put 1 tablespoon bread crumbs in each ramekin, spreading over bottom, then cover bottom and sides with slices of Swiss cheese. Top with a ½-inch thick slice of tomato and sprinkle with thyme (or basil) then add a tablespoon of cream to each. Break an egg into each ramekin, sprinkle with salt, pepper, and paprika. Add another tablespoon cream over egg and sprinkle grated Gruyère cheese over the top.

Bake in a preheated 325° F. oven uncovered until set, about

15 to 20 minutes. Serve hot with buttered whole wheat toast.
Serves 6

SOUFFLÉS AND MOUSSES

Ham-Chicken Soufflé

½ cup cooked ham, diced
½ cup cooked chicken,
  shredded
2 Tbs. butter (herbed, if
  available)
1 small onion, sliced
2 sprigs parsley, stems
  removed

1 cup Cream Sauce (below)
⅓ cup cooked carrots
¼ tsp. grated lemon rind
⅛ tsp. pulverized sage (if
  herbed butter is not used)
Salt and pepper to taste
3 eggs, separated

Put diced ham and chicken into blender with butter, sliced onion, and parsley. Add cream sauce and carrots, lemon rind, and sage, if used. Blend until smooth. Pour into saucepan and heat slowly, stirring in seasonings. When mixture starts to boil, reduce heat and add beaten egg yolks, cooking for 1 minute longer. Set aside to cool. Whip egg whites until stiff and fold lightly into cooled mixture. Pour into an ungreased soufflé dish and bake in preheated 325° F. oven about 40 minutes or until firm. Serve immediately.
Serves 5 to 6

CREAM SAUCE

3 Tbs. butter
3 Tbs. flour

1 cup chicken bouillon

Over low heat melt butter, add flour, and blend by stirring constantly for 5 to 10 minutes. Stir bouillon in slowly until smooth. Cool. For a richer sauce, use half light cream and half chicken bouillon.

Green Bean Soufflé

2 large eggs, separated
2 lbs. green or wax beans
 (or 3 9-oz. pkgs. frozen)
1/4 cup butter
1/2 cup flour (unsifted)
1 1/3 cups milk

1 tsp. salt
1/8 tsp. pepper
1 tsp. dried mint (or 1/4
 tsp. dried savory or 2
 tsps. oregano)

Let egg whites warm to room temperature for an hour in the mixer bowl. In a saucepan melt butter, remove from heat, and stir in flour until blended. Add milk slowly, stirring. Cook over low heat until smooth and thickened, stirring constantly. Add salt, pepper, and herb, stirring to blend. Let cool. Cook beans in salted water until tender, about 20 minutes, or according to package directions.

Preheat oven to 350° F. and grease well a 1½- to 2-quart soufflé dish with straight sides. Drain beans and purée in a blender at high speed for 3 to 4 minutes. Add to cool milk mixture. Beat egg yolks until thick and light. In large mixer bowl beat egg whites to form stiff peaks. Fold in yolks, bean and sauce mixture, preferably with a wire whisk. Turn into greased dish and set in a pan containing 1 inch of hot water. Bake until firm, or about 1 hour. Serve at once, hot.
Serves 6

Fish or Seafood Mousse

1 envelope unflavored
   gelatine
¼ cup cold water
¼ cup boiling water
¾ cup heavy cream
½ cup mayonnaise

3 Tbs. lemon juice
1 tsp. salt
2 cups fish or seafood,
   coarsely chopped*
Herbs†

Sprinkle gelatine into ¼ cup cold water and allow to soften for 5 minutes. Add ¼ cup boiling water; stir until dissolved. Cool.

Whip cream and combine with mayonnaise, lemon juice, salt. Gently fold in cooled gelatine and herbed fish,* using a rubber scraper or wire whisk. Turn into 1-quart mold and refrigerate for 2 hours or until firm. To unmold: run spatula around edge of mold, and invert over lettuce bed on serving dish; shake gently to release. If necessary, place hot, damp dish towel over mold, shake again to unmold.

Yield 6 to 8 servings

---

* **FISH:** Leftover cooked fish serves admirably, or fish may be baked or boiled especially for this. Canned tuna and salmon also serve; all fish must be well chopped or shredded but not too finely. Do not put in a blender or texture will be lost.

† **HERBS:** Dried or pulverized herbs are best to use so that they will mix into fish before being added to cream-mayonnaise mixture. For any fish with which tarragon is to be used, tarragon vinegar may substitute for the lemon juice. It is also possible to use Pesto alla Genovese (p. 130) without any other herbs, combining it with the mayonnaise.

   Shellfish (Shrimp precooked in garlic oil): Basil.

   Fat fish (eel, pompano, mackerel, salmon, tuna, etc.): Herbs with a stronger flavor may be used, but use sparingly. Dill, garlic, marjoram, oregano, rosemary, sage, savory, tarragon, and thyme appear in recipes for one or another of the fat fish.

   Lean fish (bluefish, cod, flounder, rockfish, sea bass, sea trout, snappers of several kinds, sole, and swordfish): Basil (for cod), dill, savory, tarragon, and thyme appear in recipes for lean fish.

   For lean and fat fish: Parsley either as flavoring or garnish proves useful. It is used especially for shellfish, while basil is used for tomato sauces that are associated with some shellfish.

CREPES, THE FRENCH PANCAKES

There are a great many basic recipes for crêpes, varying not only with the bias of the cook but also oftentimes with their use. Whether they are to be used as entrée pancakes or for dessert pancakes seems to determine the ingredients in most cases. The trick appears to be that more flour is used for main-course crêpes, while eggs are used in greater proportion to flour and liquid for dessert pancakes. No doubt you will wish to experiment and find your own ideal recipes. In general, crêpes with cream are better suited to desserts, while milk and water crêpes are more useful in the entrée course.

Crêpes may be made ahead of time, refrigerated, filled and rolled or folded over, then reheated just before serving. Or they may be filled and frozen for future use. Crêpes left over from a meal may also be frozen, of course.

Two basic recipes are given here to start you on your way.

Entrée Crêpes

6 eggs, lightly beaten	1 cup water
2 cups flour	1 cup milk
½ tsp. salt	4 Tbs. melted butter

Beat eggs in a bowl; combine salt and flour, add gradually to eggs, beating in with a wire whisk. Add liquids, about ½ cup at a time, beating well after each addition. When batter is smooth, beat in melted butter. Refrigerate for 2 to 3 hours before using.

Blender method: Combine unbeaten eggs, salt, milk, and water;

blend at medium speed for 1 minute. Add melted butter and blend. Add flour and blend at low speed 1 minute, then blend at high speed 2 minutes longer. Stop blender and scrape unblended flour from sides, then blend again briefly. Refrigerate 2 to 3 hours. Batter should be about consistency of heavy cream. Add more liquid if necessary, before refrigerating.
Yield will depend on size of pan. (About 24.)

Dessert Crêpes

6 eggs, lightly beaten
5 to 6 Tbs. all-purpose flour
4 Tbs. light cream

¼ tsp. salt
3 Tbs. melted butter
2 tsps. sugar (optional)

Beat eggs, add flour and beat in, add cream; mix salt with butter and add, beating in. Add sugar, if used. (Many people feel that sweetness in the batter ties in with sweet sauce or filling.)
Yield will depend on size of pan. (About 18.)

FILLINGS: ENTRÉE CRÊPES

Cheese Filling à l'Herbe

4 Tbs. butter
4 Tbs. all-purpose flour
2 cups milk
¼ tsp. salt
½ lb. Gruyère, diced
⅛ tsp. white pepper

¼ tsp. thyme
3 egg yolks
1 whole egg, beaten
Herbed bread crumbs (p. 186)
Oil

Melt butter in top of double boiler over boiling water; stir in flour and cook, stirring constantly, for 5 minutes. Add milk gradually, stirring the sauce with a wire whisk until thick and smooth. Add cheese, salt, pepper, and thyme; cook until cheese is melted, stirring to mix.

Remove from heat; beat in egg yolks, then pour into a buttered shallow baking pan and cool. Cut cold cheese mixture into 1½ by 3-inch pieces; place one piece on crêpe and fold over. Dip crêpes into beaten egg, then into herbed bread crumbs. Fry in deep fat at 375° F. until golden brown. Serve as luncheon entrée or as hors d'oeuvre.
Serves about 6

Seafood Filling

1 cup cooked fish (or canned crab, lobster, tuna)
2 tsps. finely chopped shallot or onion
1 Tb. butter
¼ tsp. pulverized thyme
½ tsp. salt
⅛ tsp. freshly ground black pepper
1 egg yolk
3 Tbs. bread crumbs
1½ Tbs. finely chopped parsley
1 Tb. mayonnaise

Prepare fish by cutting up or shredding. Chop onion and cook in melted butter until golden, add fish and cook lightly, mixing in the pan. Cool. Put fish mixture in a bowl and add thyme, salt, pepper, and egg yolk and mix thoroughly. Mix bread crumbs, parsley, and mayonnaise, then add to fish mixture and mix well.

Put 2 tablespoons fish mixture on one side of crêpe and roll up, starting from that side. Place in rows in a buttered shallow baking dish and drizzle a little vegetable oil over the top. Place under broiler and lightly brown, or bake until heated through.

VARIATION
Top with grated Parmesan or Gruyère cheese.

Other Fillings

Many other fillings are possible, some quite imaginative; meats, vegetables, meat-and-fruit combinations are all possibilities.

Cooked spinach, well chopped and combined with cottage cheese, a beaten egg, and perhaps a tablespoonful of grated Parmesan cheese is one method of filling, with ½ teaspoon marjoram or oregano mixed in.

Cooked ham and Gruyère or sharp Cheddar cheese, all finely diced and combined with 1 egg yolk, 3 tablespoons bread crumbs, ½ teaspoon sage, and 2 tablespoons finely chopped parsley is another possible filling mixture.

FILLINGS: DESSERT CRÊPES
(for about 12 crêpes)

Crêpes Suzette: The Sauce

½ cup butter	4 Tbs. Grand Marnier or
1 cup confectioners' sugar	curaçao
XXXX	1 Tb. grated orange rind
4 Tbs. orange juice	1 tsp. grated lemon rind
	1 Tb. lemon juice

Over a low flame melt butter, add all other ingredients, and stir. After 1 minute shut off heat, but keep sauce warm. Put 1 tablespoon on each crêpe, more if needed, to saturate it. Roll up immediately and place on heatproof dish. When all crêpes are rolled and put in a row on the dish, spoon over all 1 to 2 tablespoons curaçao or brandy, and light at table. When flames die down, serve. A bowl or a castor filled with confectioners' sugar,

THE RECIPES

to sprinkle over the crêpes, is sometimes served with the crêpes
for those with a sweeter tooth.

Apple Crêpes

3 tart apples, peeled, cored,
   diced
2 Tbs. butter
1 to 3 Tbs. sugar

Juice ½ lemon
3 Tbs. apple jelly
4 Tbs. Calvados or applejack
Additional liqueur

Cook diced apples until tender in melted butter over low heat,
add sugar (according to tartness of apples), lemon juice, and
apple jelly, and when these are well mixed, add Calvados just
before serving. Spoon 1 to 2 tablespoons mixture on each crêpe;
roll up, and put in a row on a heatproof dish. When all are
rolled, drizzle 1 to 3 tablespoons Calvados over all, light, and
serve as soon as flames die down.

Pineapple Crêpes

1½ cups canned crushed
   pineapple
½ cup granulated sugar
4 Tbs. lemon juice

1 Tb. grated lemon rind
4 Tbs. rum
Additional rum

In a saucepan combine drained pineapple, 2 tablespoons pineapple juice, sugar, lemon juice, and lemon rind. Cook over low
heat until thoroughly heated. Remove from heat and stir in rum.
Immediately spoon on each crêpe 1 to 2 tablespoons mixture,
roll up, and place on heatproof plate. When all are rolled, drizzle
over all 3 tablespoons rum, and light. When flames die, serve.

Other Fruit Fillings

Other fruits lend themselves to fillings, some simpler to prepare than the above recipes. Canned black cherries, canned plums cut in pieces, fresh or frozen sliced strawberries, and others, soaked in rum, drained, warmed in melted butter, are all good choices. Spoon two tablespoons on each crêpe, roll up and flame crêpe with rum as directed in other recipes. Other quick and easy methods for fruit fillings are below.

Thick strawberry jam. Combine with a little lemon juice and rind, warm in a small quantity of brandy, then spoon on the crêpes, which are rolled and flamed with brandy as directed in other recipes.

Pitted prunes. Soak in brandy and warm in the brandy. Roll 2 to 3 prunes in each crêpe; flame crêpes with brandy as directed in other recipes.

A quick sauce can be made by warming orange, lime, or lemon marmalade with enough fresh lemon or orange juice to dilute it a bit, adding curaçao or dark rum, filling the crêpes, and flaming them with more of the liqueur or rum.

Herbs and Crêpes

Dessert crêpes can be flavored two ways: the herb can be added to the batter or to the filling. The herb most used in fruit crêpes is mint of one kind or another. Very finely chopped mint can be added to any of the fruit fillings above, or to batter—about 2 teaspoons to 1 tablespoon, according to taste.

MEAT

Lamb Ragout

1½ lbs. lamb, cut in square
    pieces
3 medium potatoes, peeled,
    diced
3 medium onions, chopped
    coarsely
4 small carrots, sliced

1 small clove garlic, finely
    minced
Chicken stock (or bouillon)
Salt (about ½ tsp.)
Black pepper, to taste
Bouquet garni*
Chopped parsley for garnish

Put all ingredients except last two in a shallow pan. Pour over enough stock to cover, add *bouquet garni* in cheesecloth bag, cover the pan, and cook fairly briskly for 40 to 50 minutes. Remove cover the last 10 minutes if there seems to be too much liquid. Remove *bouquet garni*, put the ragout in a deep dish, and sprinkle with chopped parsley. Good served with noodles.
Serves 4 to 6

---

* Use a fresh herb **bouquet garni** made up of: 1 sprig curly parsley, 1 sprig marjoram, 1 sprig thyme, and a 2-leaf sprig of sage. If fresh herbs are not available, use a **fines herbes** mixture with both sage and thyme in it (see p. 180).

Stewed Persian Lamb with Parsley

Rumored to have come from Persia, this might as well have originated anywhere in the Near East where lamb is a staple.

3 Tbs. olive or salad oil
12 sprigs parsley, chopped

12 scallions, chopped,
    including tops

2 lbs. lean lamb, cubed
Stock (or bouillon)
Juice 2 lemons
2 Tbs. grated lemon peel

2 cups cooked kidney beans
3 Tbs. wheat germ
Salt and pepper to taste

Heat oil in casserole; sauté parsley and onions for 2 minutes, then add lamb. Pour enough stock over to cover, add lemon juice and peel, cover and simmer until lamb is very tender. Add beans, wheat germ and seasonings, and continue cooking only until beans are thoroughly heated. Serve over rice. Serves 6

VARIATION
Use only 8 scallions; add 1 clove garlic, finely minced, and 3 tablespoons finely chopped mint. Use only 1 tablespoon lemon peel.

Tomato and Meatballs
(To Be Served with Pasta)

2 Tbs. olive oil
1 medium onion, halved,
    sliced
2½ cups peeled, seeded,
    chopped tomatoes
1 Tb. coarsely chopped
    basil
1¼ lbs. ground round steak
1 large egg, beaten
1 clove garlic, pressed

2 Tbs. finely chopped
    parsley
½ cup bread crumbs,
    3 Tbs. milk
½ tsp. salt
¼ tsp. black pepper, freshly
    ground
¼ cup olive oil
Pasta
¼ cup grated Parmesan
    cheese

Heat oil in a saucepan. Separate onion slices into half rings and lightly brown in oil. Add tomatoes and basil and simmer 20 to

30 minutes. Lightly beat egg, and fork into meat, add juice of garlic, parsley, bread crumbs softened in milk, and seasonings. Mix well but lightly, then shape into very small meatballs, about the size of a walnut or smaller. Heat oil in a frying pan and fry meatballs until browned on all sides and well cooked. Remove meatballs and add to tomato mixture. Simmer for 10 minutes, then add oil from frying pan. Simmer for another 5 to 10 minutes. Serve over pasta—fine pasta, such as macaroni, or any other that suits—with Parmesan cheese to spoon over it. Or combine all in a bowl with the pasta and lightly toss.
Serves 6

Casserole of Beans au Berger

1 lb. dried red beans (or pintos)
5 cups water
½ bay leaf
2 tsps. salt
2 small cloves garlic, peeled
1 lb. chopped meat (half beef, half pork, or half lamb, half pork)
1 egg, slightly beaten
½ cup coarse bread crumbs

½ tsp. dried thyme (or marjoram)
½ tsp. dried sage (optional)
2 tsps. salt
1 can (16 oz.) tomatoes
1 tsp. dry mustard
½ cup hearty Burgundy
2 Tbs. dark-brown sugar (or blackstrap molasses)
1 Tb. butter

Wash and pick over beans. Add salt, bay leaf, and garlic to water, and when it is rapidly boiling, drop beans in gradually so as not to stop boiling. Lower heat to just above simmer and cook until beans are tender but have not burst (about 1½ hours). Remove bay leaf and garlic.

While beans cook, mix meat with egg, bread crumbs, thyme, sage (if used), and shape into walnut-sized meatballs. Melt but-

ter and brown meatballs lightly in it. Remove beans from heat when done and add salt, tomatoes, mustard, wine, and brown sugar. Mix briefly, then pour over meatballs in a 3-quart casserole and stir gently to mix. Put casserole in a preheated 350° F. oven and bake uncovered for 50 to 60 minutes or until beans are tender and done. If beans become dry while cooking, add 1 tablespoon additional butter and up to ½ cup more wine.
Serves 6 to 8

POULTRY

Chicken Livers with Sage and Wine

1 lb. chicken livers
Salt and pepper
10 to 15 leaves fresh sage,
*   well chopped (or 2 tsps.*
*   dried)*
4 slices lean bacon

1 small onion, coarsely
*   chopped*
4 Tbs. butter
⅓ cup dry white wine (or
*   sherry)*

Wash livers and cut off any tough membranes. Slice each in half. Season with salt and pepper to taste, then roll in sage until well coated. Fresh sage is preferable, but dried will suffice if well crushed or pulverized. Cut bacon into squares and fry until crisp. Drain on paper towels. Add butter to bacon fat and melt. Sauté onion until golden, then add livers and sauté for 5 to 7 minutes, add wine and simmer for 3 to 4 minutes. Serve hot with rice, buttered noodles, or polenta, with crumbled bacon over top. A ring mold can be made of rice or polenta, with center hole filled with liver mixture.
Serves 5 or 6

Deviled Broiled Chicken with Rosemary
(*Pollo alla diavolo*)

A simple and easy classic dish, well known in Rome and southern Italy, one that pales all other broiled-chicken dishes by comparison.

2 2-lb. broilers, split
5 Tbs. olive oil
Salt to taste
4 to 5 tsps. dried rosemary, well crumbled (or 3 Tbs. crushed fresh leaves)

½ cup finely chopped onion
2 Tbs. finely chopped parsley
½ cup dry white wine (or vermouth)

Wash broilers and dry with towel. Brush both sides heavily with oil, sprinkle with salt and rosemary. Place on a rack in broiling pan, skin side down. Preheat oven a few minutes then broil about 20 minutes, turn, baste, and broil for 10 minutes longer, then sprinkle with chopped onion and parsley. Broil another 10 minutes, basting with oil once or twice. When chicken is golden, remove to a hot plate. Put broiler pan on top of stove, without rack, on medium heat. Add wine, stirring it into residue in pan. As soon as it boils, scrape bottom of pan well, and pour over chicken. Served with a tossed green salad; an excellent dish for a simple supper. Use French or Italian dressing on salad.
Serves 4

Chicken Cacciatore
(*Pollo alla cacciatore*)

Originating in Italy, this was a hunter's dish, necessarily simple to prepare for obvious reasons. Yet various versions exist and some are quite complicated. A few are highly seasoned, especially those from southern Italy, while northern Italian recipes are less heavily flavored. This recipe splits the difference, adding the tomato purée of the South, while keeping pretty much to the northern ingredients for seasoning. It is a worthy, interesting, subtly fragrant dish.

5 lbs. chicken (fryers or broilers, cut in pieces)	½ tsp. freshly ground black pepper
1 large clove garlic, minced	1½ cups water
1½ cups finely chopped mild onion	½ cup tomato purée
¾ cup olive oil (or butter)	1 bay leaf
½ cup coarsely chopped parsley	1½ tsps. dried rosemary, crushed
1 cup sliced mushrooms	⅓ cup chopped fresh basil
1 tsp. salt	¾ cup red wine

In a large, heavy iron skillet sauté garlic and onion in hot oil for about 3 minutes. Add parsley and mushrooms and cook 3 to 4 minutes longer. Skim out all ingredients, then add chicken to oil and cook until golden brown. Add salt and pepper, water, tomato purée, bay leaf, rosemary, basil, and return garlic, onions, parsley, and mushrooms to skillet. Cover and simmer for about 20 minutes. Add wine and simmer uncovered for 15 to 20 minutes longer or until chicken is tender. Serve with well-buttered noodles. Juice of chicken may be spooned over them.
Serves 6 to 8

Coq au Vin
(Chicken in Claret)

There would seem to be Coq au Vin recipes by the dozen, all dear to the hearts of forty million Frenchmen. This recipe is one of the simplest to prepare, and it is at its best if prepared a day ahead and stored, covered, in the refrigerator. Heat again and let simmer for 5 minutes or so, then serve.

2 2½-lb. fryers or broilers
Flour for dredging
¼ lb. butter
½ lb. ham steak, ½ inch thick, diced
12 small white onions, peeled
½ tsp. salt
¼ tsp. black pepper, freshly ground

3 oz. brandy or cognac
2 cups claret*
Bouquet garni: 3 sprigs parsley, 2 celery tops, 1 clove garlic, peeled or halved, 1 bay leaf
2 Tbs. butter (optional)
2 Tbs. flour (optional)

Cut up chickens as for frying. Dredge pieces in flour. Melt butter in a large earthenware casserole or pan big enough to contain all chicken pieces. Sear chicken in butter and remove to a warm platter. Add diced ham and cook, stirring to sauté all sides. Add onions, salt, and pepper, and cook for 3 minutes, stirring.

Return chicken to casserole. Turn off heat. Pour brandy over chicken, light it, and allow to flambé until flames die. Add claret. If wine does not entirely cover chicken, add more, diluted half-and-half with water. Add *bouquet garni* in cheesecloth bag. Turn on heat and simmer, covered, until chicken is very tender, about 30 to 35 minutes. If casserole sauce seems watery, knead 2 tablespoons butter with 2 tablespoons flour, making small balls, and add. Cook for a few minutes more until sauce thickens. If there is excessive fat on the surface, it may be skimmed

off and discarded. Remove *bouquet garni* and serve chicken in the earthenware casserole, or place chicken on a warmed platter, arrange onions and mushrooms around it, pour sauce over it. Croutons are sometimes served with it, and parslied new potatoes, green peas, and carrots may also appear.
Serves 4 to 6

---

* If claret is not available, or if there is another dry red wine or leftover Burgundy, it may be substituted.

Chicken à la Marengo (Poulet Marengo)

Everyone seems to have a different idea of how this fine chicken dish originated. I prefer the version in LaRousse Gastronomique. *This maintains that the dish was named for the victory at Marengo, during which battle Napoleon's army outdistanced its supply train. When the famished Bonaparte demanded food (he never ate until a battle was over), his master chef Dunand was hard put to it to find anything to cook. All that turned up was a small hen, three eggs, four tomatoes, six crayfish, garlic, oil, and some bread. From these, with the addition of a little brandy (filched from Napoleon's own bottle), he created this dish. With certain additions and the crayfish deleted—the chef knew this flavor did not belong with chicken but used them because they were there—the recipe has become a classic. The eggs were fried in the oil and served around the chicken pieces. If you wish to be authentic, you may add them to the serving.*

2½- to 3-lb. chicken	2 medium onions, chopped
4 Tbs. oil	¼ lb. mushrooms, sliced
½ tsp. salt	thinly
⅛ tsp. freshly ground black	1 clove garlic, minced
pepper	2 Tbs. flour

2 Tbs. butter
½ cup consommé
¼ cup hearty red wine
¼ cup white wine

Bouquet garni: 2 sprigs
  parsley, 1 bay leaf, 1 Tb.
  chopped celery leaves
½ cup finely chopped
  parsley for garnish

Cut up chicken and brown pieces in oil. Put legs and thighs in first, since they take longer to cook. Add salt and pepper, chopped onions, mushrooms, and garlic and cook until onions are golden.

Make a *roux*—flour and melted butter mixed until smooth— in a large casserole over medium heat; stir well, add consommé, wines, and *bouquet garni* in its cheesecloth bag, with 2 tablespoons oil from chicken pan. Then add chicken mixture. Cook over low heat until tender, remove *bouquet garni*. Serve, garnished with parsley.

Serves 6

Chicken Fricassee

(Fricassée de poulet)

½ lb. new carrots
4 Tbs. butter (unsalted)
2½- to 3-lb. broiler, cut up
1 cup boiling water
Bouquet garni: 2 sprigs
    parsley, 1 sprig thyme, 2
    small stalks celery, 1
    sprig savory
1 small onion stuck with
    2 cloves

¼ lb. mushrooms, sliced
1 tsp. salt
¼ tsp. freshly ground
  pepper
5 Tbs. heavy cream
2 egg yolks, lightly beaten
Pinch sugar
Juice of 1 lemon

Wash and prepare carrots and chicken. If carrots are small, use

whole; if not, quarter them lengthwise. Fry carrots in melted butter until slightly brown and remove. Brown the pieces of chicken in pan, putting in legs and thighs first, as they take longer to cook. Add boiling water, return carrots to pan, add *bouquet garni* in cheesecloth bag, onion and mushrooms, salt and pepper. Cover and cook for 30 minutes, then remove *bouquet garni*. Pour off remaining stock and add to it cream and beaten egg yolks, sugar, and mix well. Then add lemon juice and stir well. Pour over the chicken and thoroughly warm the chicken in this sauce without bringing it to a boil. Serve hot with crisply fried croutons.
Serves 4

RABBIT

Herb-Stuffed Roast Rabbit

Adapted from an old recipe from New England, with additions from a French recipe, this rabbit is a delectable dish, whether a wild rabbit or a domestic one is the subject for stuffing.

1 small rabbit (2 lbs.)
8 to 10 slices whole wheat
  bread
4 Tbs. butter
¼ lb. mushrooms, sliced
2 Tbs. chopped onion
1 clove garlic, pressed
3 tsps. finely chopped
  marjoram (or 1 tsp. dried)
1 tsp. fresh thyme leaves
  (or ½ tsp. dried)

2 Tbs. coarsely chopped
  parsley
2 tsps. chopped fresh sage
  leaves (or ½ tsp. dried)*
⅛ tsp. nutmeg, grated
Salt to taste
¼ tsp. black pepper, freshly
  ground
1 Tb. light cream
1 egg (optional)
¼ cup white wine, or more

¼ lb. butter   2 Tbs. finely chopped
                                          parsley

Skin and prepare rabbit, skewering forelegs close to body and doubling and skewering the hind legs. Toast bread lightly. Melt butter and brush bread slices with it, then place them in a hot oven to dry completely. When dry, crumble with a rolling pin between waxed papers to make about 2 cups or more of coarse crumbs. Meantime, in butter left from brushing bread fry mushroom slices until well browned; remove. Fry onion and garlic until golden. Cool. Chop herbs (or crush dried herbs), then combine herbs, mushrooms, and onion/garlic mixture with crumbs; mix well. Add cream, and egg, if desired. (Some cooks feel that egg makes a hard dressing.) Mix well and stuff cavity of rabbit lightly, then sew edges of skin together to retain stuffing.

Braise the rabbit in the wine in a large skillet, then lower the heat to just above simmer and cook covered for 2 hours or until tender, turning frequently. Melt the ¼ lb. butter and add 2 tablespoons parsley. Use to baste the rabbit frequently during cooking time, and add a little more wine, sparingly, if it cooks away too much and rabbit seems likely to scorch. About 15 to 20 minutes before serving, transfer rabbit to a broiler pan and brown in the oven at 350° F., turning to brown both sides evenly.

Serves 6 to 8

---

* Sage is usually used for wild rabbit, infrequently with domestic rabbit. A more highly seasoned dressing will result from its use.

Rabbit Braised with Herbs

2 small rabbits (1½ to 2 lbs. each)
4 thick slices lean bacon
4 Tbs. chopped onion
1 cloves garlic, pressed
3 Tbs. olive oil
3 sprigs parsley, chopped
½ tsp. dried basil (or 2 Tbs. fresh, chopped)
½ tsp. dried marjoram (or 2 Tbs. fresh, chopped)
4 large tomatoes, sliced or 1 can (16 oz.)
1 tsp. salt
¼ tsp. black pepper, freshly ground
⅔ cup hearty red wine

Prepare rabbits, rinse in cold water, and pat dry. Cut into pieces. Fry bacon in a large casserole until crisp, remove, drain, and cool. In same pan add onion and garlic juice and fry until golden. Remove. Place rabbit in pan and sauté until nicely browned on all sides. Remove pan from heat, add remaining ingredients, and mix well. Put back on heat and bring to boiling, reduce heat, and cover. Simmer for 45 minutes to 1 hour or until rabbit is tender. Place pieces of rabbit on a heated plate, spoon juices over it and serve.

Serves 6 to 8

SAUCES

Pesto alla Genovese

This memorable green sauce that gracefully seasons pasta, sometimes appears also in minestrone or other soups, or flavors gnocchi di patate, *has many versions. In fact, there are so many* individual versions as well as regional ones that the field may be wide open for further experimentation. A few tips may help. For instance, add a little salt to the basil leaves to help preserve the green color. Some Italians add a bit of butter to make the paste smoother. Whenever there is leftover pesto, put it in a jar, spoon over it a little olive oil, and tightly seal before storing it in the refrigerator for use later. If you make the pesto a day or night in advance of use, reserve a tablespoonful of oil and top with it, storing as above. Mix it in well, of course, before using.

5 to 6 cloves of garlic,
   minced
2 cups fresh basil leaves
½ tsp. salt

6 Tbs. freshly grated
   Parmesan cheese
½ cup olive oil

Crush in a mortar all ingredients except oil until a smooth paste is achieved. Then, adding a few drops of oil at a time, stir it in until the green paste is thick and smooth.

Blender method: Reserve oil but blend all other ingredients at high speed until paste forms, then lower speed to medium and add oil in a slow trickle, blending thoroughly.

Yield: about ¾ to 1 cup

VARIATIONS

Add ⅓ cup chopped pine nuts or walnuts, crushing in mortar.

Use 1½ cups basil and ½ cup chopped parsley.

Add 1 teaspoon tomato paste to *pesto* when using with minestrone. This makes canned minestrone individual and more palatable.

Add 1 tablespoon unsalted butter to sauce when blending. Or just before use, add 1 tablespoon butter and 1 to 1½ tablespoons boiling water. Mix.

Mint Sauce, Cold

½ *cup minced fresh mint*
   leaves

1 *cup cider* (*or distilled*)
   vinegar
2 *or* 3 *Tbs. sugar*

Wash and pick over mint, removing leaves from stems. Chop well and put in a saucepan. Dissolve sugar in vinegar, then pour over mint and place over a stove burner that has been heated and then turned off. Infuse for an hour or so, then cool. A pinch or two of salt may be added before infusion, if desired.
Yield: 1½ cups

Mint Sauce, Hot

½ *cup minced fresh mint*
   leaves
½ *cup lemon juice*
½ *cup lime juice*

1 *cup sugar*
½ *cup water*
⅛ *tsp. salt*

Wash and pick over mint, removing leaves from stems. Chop well and put in a saucepan. Blend lemon and lime juices with sugar, water, and salt in a small saucepan and put over a low heat to cook for 5 minutes, stirring to dissolve sugar. Do not boil. Add mint leaves, stir, turn off heat, and allow to stand on cooling burner for 10 to 15 minutes. Reheat and serve hot. Store in a tightly stoppered bottle.
Yield: 1½ cups

Orange and Lemon Mint Sauce

½ cups minced fresh mint
   leaves
½ cup fresh orange juice
½ cup fresh lemon juice
1½ tsps. grated orange peel

1½ tsps. grated lemon peel
¼ tsp. salt
2½ Tbs. confectioners' sugar
⅛ tsp. nutmeg
⅛ tsp. powdered cinnamon

Combine all ingredients and stir to mix well. Put in a double boiler or a bowl over hot water and infuse for a half hour, stirring occasionally. Serve hot with lamb, venison, or other game.
Yield: about 1¼ to 1⅓ cups

Quick Mint Sauce

¼ cup minced fresh mint
   leaves

1 cup Minted Sweet Vinegar
   (below)
¼ tsp. salt

Wash and pick over mint, remove leaves from stem and mince. Put in a saucepan. Heat Minted Sweet Vinegar over low flame until hot, but do not boil. Pour over mint and let stand until cool, or let stand 10 minutes and serve hot.
Yield: 1 cup

Minted Sweet Vinegar

2½ cups minced fresh mint
   leaves

1 quart cider vinegar
1 cup sugar

Wash and pick over mint, remove leaves from stems and chop

fine. Bring vinegar to boiling point in an enamel saucepan over medium heat. Add sugar and mint leaves. Reduce heat and simmer 5 minutes. Remove from heat and strain immediately through fine mesh sieve. Pour vinegar into hot sterilized bottle while still very hot and cork tightly. Can be used in preparing mint sauces, as above, in flavoring dressings for fruit salads, and in cookery where vinegar is called for and mint flavoring is desirable.

Yield: about 1 quart

Multi-Herb Sauce

2 oz. butter
1 shallot, minced
½ tsp. marjoram, minced (or ⅛ tsp. dried)
½ tsp. finely chopped parsley
½ tsp. finely chopped sage (or ⅛ tsp. dried, pulverized)

½ tsp. minced fresh thyme (or ⅛ dried, pulverized)
3 tsps. finely chopped celery
¾ cup red wine vinegar*
Salt and pepper to taste
2 Tbs. olive or salad oil

Melt butter in saucepan over moderate heat, add chopped shallot (minced green onion may be substituted), and sauté gently for 4 minutes. Add herbs and celery, and pour vinegar over all. Simmer over low heat for about 10 minutes, then add seasonings to taste, blending in oil last. Serve hot over beef or veal.

Yield: about 1 cup

---

* For fish or chicken dishes, substitute white wine vinegar.

Herbed Curry Sauce

2 oz. butter
2 medium onions, finely
  chopped
4 short stalks celery, minced
1 carrot, thinly sliced
½ tsp. salt
⅛ tsp. white pepper

1 tsp. ground dried thyme
1 Tb. parsley, finely
  minced
1 tsp. curry powder
2 cups chicken broth
1½ Tbs. flour
1 Tb. butter

Melt butter over medium heat, add onion, carrot, celery, salt, and pepper and sauté until vegetables are soft, about 15 minutes. Add thyme, parsley, curry powder, and broth and stir well. In a small amount of water mix flour until smooth and add to saucepan, stirring and cooking for about 5 or 6 minutes more. Remove from heat and strain through sieve. Reheat sauce, add 1 tablespoon butter and mix it in as it melts. Serve sauce very hot with fish, shellfish, chicken, eggs, or vegetables.
Yield: about 2 cups for 6 or more servings

Wine Sauce with Shallots

1 cup dry white wine
1 Tb. tarragon vinegar
1½ Tbs. finely chopped
  shallots
3 Tbs. finely chopped
  parsley
2 tsps. finely chopped
  tarragon

1 tsp. sugar (optional)
Few grains cayenne pepper
¼ tsp. salt
3 egg yolks
4 Tbs. sweet butter
1½ Tbs. tomato paste
½ cup coffee cream

Place wine, vinegar, shallots, parsley, tarragon, sugar, salt, and

135

cayenne in a saucepan, stir well and bring to a boil over high heat. Reduce heat and boil gently until liquid is reduced to about half, about 20 to 25 minutes. Remove from heat and cool a few minutes before straining through a fine-mesh sieve. Place strained liquid in top of a double boiler over boiling water and beat in 1 egg yolk at a time alternately with 1 tablespoon butter. Stir in remaining butter, then add tomato paste and cream, stirring until fully blended. Serve very hot with roast veal and poultry or over boiled, broiled, or baked fish.
Yield: about 1 cup

Mint Butter Sauce

½ cup butter	⅛ tsp. salt (optional)
2 Tbs. lemon juice	⅓ cup finely chopped mint

Mix butter with a spoon in a shallow bowl until soft. Add lemon juice about 1 teaspoon at a time with salt (if butter is unsalted). When well mixed, add mint and again mix thoroughly. Chill slightly and serve with hot lamb or over carrots.
Yield: about ¾ cup

Ravigote Butter Sauce

2 shallots	1½ tsps. finely chopped chives
1½ tsps. finely chopped tarragon	1 tsp. capers, finely chopped
1½ tsps. finely chopped parsley	¼ cup butter
	¼ tsp. salt (optional)

Chop shallots, herbs and capers. Then cream butter in a bowl until soft. Gradually add herbs and mix into butter. Use salt if butter is unsalted. Green coloring matter may be added if desired. Serve chilled for use on hot boiled meats, fish, shellfish, or vegetables.

Yield: ¼ cup or more

Herb Butter Sauce

2 Tbs. finely chopped fresh leaves (parsley, chives, basil, or other herbs singly or combined)

½ cup butter
1 Tb. flour
2 Tbs. milk
⅛ tsp. salt (optional)

Wash and lightly dry herb leaves; chop. In top of a double boiler, over boiling water, melt butter. If salted butter is used, omit salt. Mix flour, milk, and salt to smoothness, then add to butter and stir until smooth and hot. Serve hot.

Yield: about ⅔ cup

Parsley Butter Sauce

½ cup butter
2 Tbs. finely chopped parsley

⅛ tsp. salt (optional)
⅛ tsp. paprika

Melt butter in top of double boiler over boiling water. Add parsley, salt (unless butter is salted), and paprika. Keep warm for about 5 minutes and serve hot.

Yield: ½ cup

Onion-Tomato Sauce

½ cup olive oil
1 or 2 cloves garlic, finely
   minced
2 large onions, finely
   chopped

6 large or 8 medium-sized
   ripe tomatoes (or 3 to 4
   cups canned tomatoes)
6 to 8 leaves basil
Salt and pepper to taste

Heat oil in a large skillet to verge of smoking; fry onions until golden, then add garlic and cook a minute more. Add tomatoes (skinned, seeded, and chopped), basil, salt, and pepper, then turn down heat and simmer until sauce has thickened as liquid evaporates (about 10 to 15 minutes). If tomatoes are on acid side, add ½ teaspoonful sugar. Sauce should be as thick as heavy cream.

Yield: 3½ to 4 cups

Green Parsley Sauce

1 medium potato, boiled
1 small clove garlic
5 to 7 sprigs curly parsley
2 Tbs. olive oil

2 tsps. wine vinegar
1 Tb. white wine
Salt and pepper to taste
3 to 5 Tbs. beef bouillon

Blender: Cut potato into cubes and put it with all other ingredients into a blender. Blend at moderate speed. If too thick, add a little more bouillon.

Mortar: Mash and blend in a mortar: potato, garlic, and parsley; then blend in gradually: olive oil, vinegar, and wine. Add salt and pepper, and beef bouillon, sparingly, until desired consistency is reached.

Yield: about ½ to ¾ cup

Sauce Rémoulade

1 cup mayonnaise
1 Tb. finely chopped basil
 leaves
1 Tb. finely chopped scallions
 (green part also)
1 large clove garlic, crushed
 and juice only used

1 Tb. finely chopped fresh
 tarragon
1 Tb. finely chopped parsley
1 Tb. Dijon mustard (or 1
 tsp. dry mustard)
1 tsp. well-chopped capers
2 gherkins, finely chopped
Anchovy oil (optional)

Combine all ingredients and serve with fish dishes: grilled or broiled fish, shrimp, lobster, crab. For these, add oil from a small can of anchovies when mixing.

For serving with pork dishes, especially cold pork chops, ham, etc., omit anchovy oil.

Yield: about 1½ to 1¾ cups

NOTE
An herb-flavored mayonnaise may be used. In such case, omit any ingredients listed that were used in mayonnaise.

Sauce Vinaigrette (see French Dressing)

Sauce Rouge (Red Mayonnaise)

⅔ cup mayonnaise
3 Tbs. tomato purée
2 tsps. finely chopped basil
 (or scant ½ tsp. dried)
6 to 8 small beets (canned)

¼ tsp. salt
⅛ tsp. freshly ground black
 pepper
Pinch of sugar
Paprika

Chop basil, dice beets; place in blender with other ingredients and add mayonnaise; blend at low speed for 3 minutes.

If sauce is being used for tomato dishes, omit beets and double tomato purée. An especially decorative use is for eggs in a ring mold, either baked or in aspic. Fill center of ring with *sauce rouge*. The ring mold of Eggs in Aspic (p. 88) can be turned out on a dish, with *sauce verte* (below) piped about it and the center filled with *sauce rouge*. Sprinkle paprika over sauce.
Yield: about 1½ cups

Sauce Verte (Green Mayonnaise)

⅔ cup mayonnaise (herb-
flavored)
2 Tbs. coarsely chopped
parsley
3 Tbs. coarsely chopped
watercress

½ tsp. salt
1 Tb. finely chopped
tarragon
1 Tb. finely chopped chives
Juice ½ lemon
Pinch sugar

Wash and pick over herbs, discard heavy stems of parsley and any watercress stems that seem woody. Chop and measure. If tarragon mayonnaise is used, omit chopped fresh tarragon. Put all in blender and add mayonnaise, blending at moderate speed for 2 minutes. Serve with fish dishes, shellfish, and with certain egg dishes.
Yield: about 1¼ to 1½ cups

Sauce Tartare

1 cup mayonnaise
1 Tb. finely chopped onion
1 Tb. finely chopped capers
1 Tb. finely chopped chives
1 Tb. coarsely chopped
  gherkins
Salt and pepper to taste

Optional additions:
  2 tsps. finely chopped
    parsley
  2 tsps. finely chopped
    tarragon
  ½ clove garlic, finely minced
  1 Tb. finely chopped
    shallots (to replace onion)
  Pinch sugar

Combine ingredients, chill in refrigerator. Serve with grilled and poached fish, with all kinds of shellfish, and with seafood salad. Salad should be dressed and tossed with French dressing, *sauce tartare* passed to be added.
Yield: 1½ cups

Rhine-Wine Sauce

Often a little wine is left over after a dinner and the question arises whether to drink it or dispose of it. Leftover white wine can be put to good use in a sauce, either Rhine wine, as called for here, or substituting another good white wine.

2 Tbs. capers
½ tsp. dried dill weed
1 Tb. grated onion
2 Tbs. finely minced parsley
10 green olives, chopped

¼ tsp. salt
⅛ tsp. white pepper
¼ cup Rhine wine
1 cup mayonnaise (p. 161)

Put all ingredients except mayonnaise in the top of a double boiler over boiling water and stir gently to combine for a minute or two. Add mayonnaise, and turn down heat; stir well to combine until heated through, 8 to 10 minutes. Serve piping hot. Excellent with fish, baked or steamed, especially salmon, whitefish, and sole.

Yield: about 1½ cups

NOTE

All ingredients can be placed in a blender and thoroughly blended, then heated for serving.

Five-Herb Wine Sauce

4 Tbs. butter
1 shallot, finely chopped
1 tsp. each, fresh, finely
  chopped: parsley (½ tsp.
  dried), thyme (⅛ tsp. dried),
  marjoram (¼ tsp. dried),
  sage (⅛ tsp. dried), savory
  (¼ tsp. dried)

⅔ cup white wine (or cider
  vinegar)
Salt to taste
Black pepper, freshly
  ground to taste
2 Tbs. olive oil

Melt butter in a saucepan over medium heat, add shallot and sauté for 3 minutes. Add herbs, wine or vinegar, and simmer for 10 minutes. Add seasoning and olive oil and blend well.

Serve hot over boiled beef, roast chicken, baked fish, or roast veal. For roast pork, substitute ⅛ teaspoon rosemary for savory.

Yield: about 1 cup

Apple-Horseradish Sauce

1 lb. tart apples
¼ cup white wine vinegar

¼ tsp. lemon thyme (dried,
  pulverized)

2 Tbs. sugar   1 Tb. lemon juice
2 Tbs. prepared horseradish
  (or fresh, grated)

Peel, core, and grate apples and immediately combine with pre-
viously prepared vinegar—vinegar heated just to boiling with
thyme and sugar. Add horseradish and lemon juice, and add
more sugar if sauce is too tart. Mix well and store in refrigerator
in tightly covered jar. Good with roast lamb and pork, also with
goose or duck. If lemon thyme is not available, use common
thyme and add ½ teaspoon grated lemon peel.
Yield: about 2 cups

Applesauce with Mint

3 Tbs. chopped mint   ¼ tsp. salt
⅔ cup water   ⅓ to ½ cup sugar
6 apples

Bring water to boil, add mint, and boil for 1 minute. Turn off
heat and let mint cool in water. Peel, core, and chop apples;
sieve mint water and put with apples into a saucepan. Cover,
simmer gently until almost soft, then add salt and sugar. If
apples are tart, more sugar may be needed. If apples are too
bland, add 1 teaspoon lemon juice. Simmer gently until moisture
is reduced and applesauce is thickened.

VARIATIONS
   Add ½ cupful raisins with sugar. Or soak raisins in white
wine, drain, and add with sugar.

143

VEGETABLES

Herbed Stewed Tomatoes

6 large tomatoes (3½ cups
   canned)
3 Tbs. butter
¼ cup (or more) dry bread
   crumbs

1 Tb. brown sugar
1 tsp. dried basil (or 2 Tbs.
   fresh, finely chopped)
Salt and pepper

Pour boiling water over tomatoes to cover, let stand 1 minute, then drain and cover with cold water. Remove skins and stem; quarter and chop coarsely. Put tomatoes with all other ingredients in an enamel saucepan and bring to a boil. Reduce heat and simmer over low heat until tomatoes are tender, about 8 to 10 minutes.

NOTE
   Omit basil and use ½ to 1 teaspoon dried thyme, pulverized, as a variation when serving tomatoes as a side dish with pork. Serves 6 to 8

Tomatoes Stuffed with Herbed Rice

8 large ripe tomatoes
1 cup rice
½ cup chicken stock or
   broth
1 Tb. finely chopped
   parsley
1 Tb. olive oil

1 tsp. salt
¼ tsp. black pepper, freshly
   ground
1 tsp. dried basil (or 3 Tbs.
   fresh, finely chopped)
Roquefort cheese
Parsley sprigs for garnish

144

Tomatoes must be firm, though ripe. Cut off about ½ inch of top (stem end) and scoop out seeds and pulp, reserving them. Prepare rice, drain, and return to saucepan. Add chicken stock or broth, parsley, oil, salt, and pepper, and ½ teaspoon basil. Stir in the reserved tomato seeds and pulp. Bring to a boil, turn down heat, and simmer about 15 minutes or until rice is nicely soft. In each drained tomato cavity put a small lump (about ½ to ¾ tsp.) of Roquefort cheese (American blue cheese will also serve) and sprinkle with remainder of basil. Lightly fill tomatoes with stuffing, mounding it up in the center. Bake in a preheated 350° F. oven for 25 to 30 minutes or until browned. Serve hot. Serves 4 to 8

Tomato and Corn Casserole

4 tomatoes, large, ripe
2 Tbs. butter
2 Tbs. flour
1¼ cups milk
¼ tsp. pulverized thyme
Salt and pepper to taste

1 cup canned whole-kernel corn (12 oz.)
3 Tbs. finely chopped parsley
Sliced aged Cheddar cheese
¼ cup fine bread crumbs
2 Tbs. butter

Pour boiling water over tomatoes to cover, let stand 1 minute, drain, and cover with cold water. Remove skins and cut into thick slices. Melt butter in a small saucepan, blend flour in it until smooth, add milk, thyme, and seasonings and stir constantly over low heat until mixture thickens to a white sauce.

Butter a large casserole and put about half the corn in the bottom. Pour half the thickened sauce over this layer, then add a layer of tomato slices. Use remaining corn for a layer, then top with remaining tomatoes and white sauce. Arrange slices of

cheese over tomatoes and top with bread crumbs. Dot with butter. Bake about 25 minutes in a 350° F. oven or until casserole is cooked through and cheese begins to bubble.
Serves 6

Herb-Stuffed Baked Potatoes
(*Pommes de terre farce aux herbes*)

6 large Idaho baking potatoes	*2 Tbs. finely chopped parsley*
3 Tbs. butter	*2 egg yolks*
½ tsp. salt	*Paprika (optional)*
¼ tsp. white pepper	*3 Tbs. grated Gruyère cheese*
¼ cup hot milk	

Choose potatoes of uniform size, scrub, rinse, and dry them. Place on rack in oven. (If desired, rub with oil for a softer skin before putting in oven.) Bake 40 to 60 minutes at 450° F. Pick up with a heavy cloth and squeeze to test doneness. When soft, they are done; if not, return for further cooking.

Cut a slice off side of potato, scoop out pulp and discard skin. Scoop out pulp from rest of potato, reserve this skin. Mash pulp thoroughly or put through a ricer. Add butter, salt, pepper, and milk. Beat until light and fluffy, then add egg yolks, parsley, and cheese. Mix thoroughly. Lightly fill reserved potato skins with the mixture, heaping it slightly. Put in a greased shallow baking pan or on a greased baking sheet and dust tops with paprika, or sprinkle lightly with cheese. Bake at 375° F. for 5 to 10 minutes or until lightly browned on top and heated through. Garnish with a sprig of parsley.
Serves 6

VARIATIONS

Add 1 teaspoon finely chopped onion with parsley, or substitute chives for parsley.

To ¼ cup grated Parmesan cheese add 3 hard-cooked egg yolks, coarsely sieved, and mix with potato. Fill skins, lightly brush tops with melted butter and sprinkle paprika over them.

To 2 tablespoons minced watercress add 2 teaspoons finely chopped mint leaves and mix with potatoes. Do not garnish with parsley.

Discard potato skins. Shape mixture into flat ovals between two greased tablespoons. Bake in 375° F. oven about 20 minutes on a well-greased baking sheet until lightly browned.

Mixture can also be placed in a greased casserole. Reserve some and force through a pastry tube to make a fancy border (as for duchesse potatoes) around the rim and to decorate the middle. Bake in 375° F. oven about 20 minutes or until lightly browned.

Overstuffed Zucchini

6 zucchini (medium, 8 in.)	½ tsp. dried oregano, or 1 sprig fresh, chopped
2 to 3 strips lean bacon	
1 cup chopped onion	2½ Tbs. grated Parmesan cheese
1 Tb. butter or margarine	
1 Tb. flour	½ tsp. salt
¼ cup undiluted consommé (canned)	¼ tsp. black pepper, freshly grated
¼ cup milk or thin yoghurt	1 Tb. grated Parmesan cheese (additional)
½ cup dry bread crumbs	
1 Tb. chopped parsley	

Preheat oven to 450°F. Grease well a shallow casserole or baking dish large enough to contain zucchini side by side.

Cut off both ends of zucchini and discard. Slice about a third off one side of each zucchini, then put slices and other zucchini in a pan of boiling salted water. Reduce heat, simmer until tender (about 7 to 9 minutes), and drain.

Scoop out pulp from slices and discard skin. Scoop out pulp from other zucchini, leaving enough to support the skins and ends. Chop well all pulp, then place in a sieve to drain. Press pulp lightly between paper towels to dry still more.

Fry bacon until very crisp; cool and crumble it. In bacon fat (add a little butter if needed), sauté onion until golden. Add zucchini pulp and simmer over a low flame. Make a white sauce with 1 tablespoon butter and 1 tablespoon flour, stirring as it cooks until it bubbles. Add consommé and milk or yoghurt, stirring constantly until sauce thickens; then cook 1 minute more, letting it bubble. Add sauce to onion and pulp, stir in bread crumbs, parsley, oregano, Parmesan cheese, seasonings, and crumbled bacon. Mix well. Spoon into zucchini shells and arrange them side by side in casserole. Sprinkle additional Parmesan cheese over all. Bake at 450° F. for 10 to 15 minutes, until tops begin to brown. Serve hot with a wedge of lemon, if desired.

Serves 6

Green Beans aux Herbes

1 lb. green beans, or 1 pkg. (10 oz.) frozen beans
1/3 to 1/2 cup boiling water
1/2 tsp. salt
1 sprig fresh savory (or 1 tsp. dried, pulverized)

4 slices Canadian bacon or 6 of regular bacon
2 Tbs. butter, melted
1/3 cup finely chopped onion
2 Tbs. finely chopped parsley

1 tsp. dried marjoram (or 3
  tsps. fresh, finely
  chopped)

Small pinch dried, pulverized
  rosemary
½ tsp. black pepper, freshly
  ground

Prepare beans, cut across or French style. Add savory to salted boiling water, then add beans; cover pot, simmer gently 15 to 20 minutes, checking occasionally and adding more water lightly if too much has evaporated. Drain and keep beans warm. (*Frozen beans:* cook according to package directions but in a little less water.)

Cut bacon in quarters; fry until crisp, drain, and when cool, chop. In melted butter cook onion until golden, then add herbs and seasonings; add beans and stir. Heat through before turning into serving dish. Sprinkle top with chopped bacon.

Serves 4

VARIATION

For herbs in this recipe substitute ½ teaspoon dried Fines Herbes Blend, Classic (p. 181) or for Vegetables (p. 181).

Baked Eggplant with Cheese
(*Melanzane Parmigiana*)

An Italian recipe that can be made into a splendid main course or used to accompany a meat course, thus serving more people at dinner or at a hearty midday meal. It is good served hot, warm, or even cold, but not refrigerated.

1 large or 2 small eggplants
Salt

4 cups canned stewed
  tomatoes (or fresh,
  blanched, peeled, chopped)

2 small onions, finely
  chopped
5 Tbs. olive oil
1 clove garlic, finely minced
2 tsps. dried, or 3 sprigs
  chopped fresh basil
½ tsp. salt

¼ tsp. freshly ground black
  pepper
4 Tbs. olive oil
Flour
Parmesan cheese, grated
10 oz. mozzarella cheese
4 hard-cooked eggs, sliced
1½ cups fine bread crumbs

Cut stem end off eggplant, then slice lengthwise about ⅜ inch thick. Sprinkle with salt and arrange in layers in a large bowl. Cover with ice water, and put a weighted plate on top to keep them submerged while bitter juices soak out. After 1 hour remove slices from salty water and wash, then pat dry with paper towels. Prepare tomatoes, if fresh, and set aside. Chop onions, heat olive oil in a heavy frying pan, fry onions and the garlic until golden, then add tomatoes and basil. Mix well and simmer gently, uncovered, until sauce becomes thickened. Season with salt and pepper.

Preheat oven to 400° F. Put olive oil in a large flat casserole. Dredge slices of eggplant with flour and fry until soft in the olive oil; set aside on hot plate or in warmed oven. When all are fried, leave enough slices on bottom of casserole to cover it completely without overlapping. Sprinkle with Parmesan cheese, then arrange a layer of mozzarella cheese, a thin layer of bread crumbs, with egg slices on top. Spoon tomato sauce over this layer, then repeat layers in same order until all ingredients are used. Top with a layer of bread crumbs and a sprinkling of Parmesan cheese. Bake uncovered in oven for ½ hour or until sauce bubbles and cheese begins to melt. Remove from oven and allow about 10 minutes before serving.

Serves 6 to 8

Green Beans au Jambon Julienne

1 lb. fresh green beans, or
 1 pkg. (10 oz.) frozen
 green beans
1/3 to 1/2 cup boiling water
1/2 tsp. salt
 1 Tb. butter, melted
1/4 cup finely chopped onions
 2 oz. ham, cut in strips*
 2 Tbs. finely chopped
 parsley

1/4 tsp. dried, pulverized
 marjoram
Small pinch dried, pulverized
 rosemary
 6 to 8 black olives, pitted
 and chopped
3/4 tsp. salt
1/8 to 1/4 tsp. black pepper,
 freshly ground

Prepare beans, cut across or French style, and add to boiling salted water. Cover pot and simmer gently over low heat for 15 to 20 minutes, checking occasionally to see if a little more water is needed. Drain beans and keep warm. (*Frozen beans:* Cook according to package directions but use a little less water than directed.)

Cut ham into strips 2 inches long by 1/4 inch wide. Sauté onions in melted butter until golden (about 5 minutes), then add ham strips and cook over lowered heat for 2 minutes or less. Add balance of ingredients and the beans, stirring gently to mix. When thoroughly heated through, turn into a warmed serving dish.

Serves 4

---

* Either leftover ham, canned ham, or sliced boiled ham may be used.

Herbed Dried White Beans

2 cups dried white beans
1 medium onion

1 carrot
1 clove garlic, peeled

1 sprig thyme (or savory)   1 tsp. salt, or to taste
2 cloves   1 tsp. salt butter, or more

Wash beans in cold water and pick over, discarding any damaged or imperfect ones. Place in casserole with onion into which cloves have been stuck, carrot scraped but not peeled, garlic, and sprig of herb. Cover with boiling water to about 2 inches above beans. Cover casserole and cook over low heat until beans are tender (1½ to 3 hours). Beans should simmer, not boil hard, and should be tender, not mushy. Drain thoroughly, remove and discard cloved onion, carrot, herb sprig, and garlic. Do not salt until beans have been cooked, then mix well, put butter on top and serve. Pass a good hot tomato sauce to spoon over beans (see p. 138).
Serves 4

Pinto Beans with Sage

2 cups pinto beans   1 tsp. salt
6 cups boiling water   ¼ tsp. black pepper, freshly
½ lb. slab bacon or salt   ground
   pork, cubed   ½ tsp. dry mustard
1 large onion, chopped   1 tsp. dried, pulverized sage
1 clove garlic (optional)   2 Tbs. dark honey

Wash and pick over beans and put in saucepan. Pour over them the boiling water and let stand, covered, 2 hours. Cook cubed bacon or pork until lightly browned, remove from fat and add to beans; pour off fat except for about 4 teaspoonfuls; cook onion in it until golden, then add to beans. If garlic is used, cook with onion. Using enough tepid water to form a thin mixture, stir

together salt, pepper, mustard, sage, and honey. Add to beans, then cover pan and boil gently over moderate heat for about 2 hours or until tender; add more water if needed, but beans should not be watery when served.
Serves 4

Dried Black Beans Baked with Herbs

2 cups dried black beans (or
   red kidney beans)
2 tsps. salt
1 clove garlic, peeled
2 leaves fresh sage, or
   ¼ tsp. dried, pulverized
Boiling water
½ tsp. dried, pulverized
   marjoram
½ tsp. dried, pulverized
   thyme

Pinch pulverized rosemary
2 medium onions, sliced
⅔ tsp. salt
¼ tsp. black pepper, freshly
   ground
2 to 3 oz. bacon, or leftover
   ham, diced or cut up
½ cup red wine
1 Tb. wine vinegar
3 tsps. butter

Wash and pick over beans. In 4 to 5 cups rapidly boiling water place garlic and sage, then gradually drop in beans so that water never stops boiling. Turn down heat when all beans are in pot and simmer until beans are tender but have not burst (1 hour or longer). Remove garlic and sage leaves, then put beans and bean water in a bean pot, adding additional water as needed to cover beans. Stir in all other ingredients except wine, vinegar, and butter. In uncovered pot, bake in preheated 250° F. oven 1½ hours, stirring occasionally and adding more water if needed. Stir in wine, vinegar, and butter 10 minutes before serving, mixing well over low heat to help assimilate flavors.
Serves 4 or more

Lentil Loaf

2 slices bacon, crisped,
  chopped
2½ cups boiled lentils
  1 cup cooked kasha (or
    millet)
  1 egg, beaten
  ½ tsp. salt
  2 medium onions, grated

1 clove garlic, finely
  minced
¼ tsp. dried thyme,
  pulverized
2 Tbs. finely minced parsley
3 Tbs. wheat germ
1 Tb. finely chopped chives
Milk

Blend all ingredients, adding only enough milk to make moist enough to mold. Place in a well-greased loaf pan and bake for 40 to 45 minutes at 375° F. Serve sliced, with a sauce, perhaps a tomato sauce (p. 138).
Serves 6

Lentil-Soybean Loaf

1 cup lentils, boiled
1 cup soybeans, boiled
1 cup brown or wild rice,
  boiled
2 cups milk
¼ cup soybean grits
1½ Tbs. finely chopped mint

2 Tbs. finely chopped
  parsley
3 scallions, minus green,
  chopped
½ to ¾ cup bouillon
3 Tbs. wheat germ

Cook lentils, soybeans, and rice, using boiling water to reduce preparation time. Drain when tender. Meantime, soak soy grits in milk for about 1 hour. Combine all ingredients, mix well, adding more bouillon if mixture is too tight. Place in a well-greased pan and bake for 30 to 35 minutes at 350° F.
Serves 6

Baked Soybeans

4 cups soybeans, boiled
1 large carrot, grated
1 medium onion, grated
½ cup celery tops, chopped
3 Tbs. chopped green
   pepper
1 Tb. tomato purée

4 Tbs. blackstrap molasses
¼ tsp. sage, crumbled
1 tsp. oregano
3 Tbs. finely minced parsley
¼ cup cooked ham, diced
Tomato juice (about 6 oz.)

Mix all ingredients except tomato juice in a large bowl, then pour into a well-greased casserole. Pour on about ⅓ of the tomato juice, and bake, covered, in preheated oven at 350° F. for 1¾ to 2 hours. After 1¼ hours remove cover and add more tomato juice; check from time to time, adding more juice as necessary to keep the beans moist. If more than 6 ounces of tomato juice are needed, do not stint.
Serves 6 to 8

Herbed Soybean Casserole

2 cups boiled soybeans
2 cups cooked sweet corn
   (frozen may be sub-
   stituted for fresh)
2 cups chopped fresh or
   canned tomatoes
⅓ cup grated Parmesan
   cheese

¼ cup salad oil
3 Tbs. finely chopped
   parsley
½ tsp. sage, crumbled
¼ cup beef bouillon
¼ cup fine bread crumbs
Wheat germ

Into a well-greased casserole put a layer of beans, one of corn, one of tomatoes, and sprinkle cheese over all. Repeat until all ingredients are in casserole. Mix oil, herbs, and bouillon, then pour over casserole. Cover and bake at 350° F. for 30 to 35 minutes. Remove cover at 25 minutes, sprinkle bread crumbs mixed with wheat germ over the top, and let bake remaining time.

Serves 6 to 8

OF SALADS AND SANITY

You must forgive me if I sound somewhat rabid on the subject of salads. At an early, impressionable age I was exposed to many so-called salads, and I still shudder at the pictures evoked by the memory. Later on I was to encounter what is prevalent to-day, that red glue, slow-flowing and viscous, that is foisted on the American public as "French Dressing." The combination of these two unhappy circumstances accounts for my bias. Perhaps you will agree with me if you will taste the results of my experience with salads and sharpen your taste buds (or should I say bring them into bloom?) as you do so.

The salads of my childhood were served by family friends who wanted to show off the knowledge acquired from "ladies' magazines" or possibly invented by those who were more adventurous than experienced in taste. One such salad stands out. Even as a child I realized that the ingredients were somehow off-key, yet all those at the dinner adopted it, for we were served that salad for years at the homes of various friends. It was a Butterfly Salad, composed of a limp, round lettuce leaf (possibly cut round with pinking shears), on which was placed a quarter banana (sliced lengthwise and then crosswise) for the body, flanked by two half slices of pineapple for wings. A rounded spoonful of cottage cheese filled each hole in the wing and another spoonful served as a head to hold in place a giant olive, which had two stuffed olive slices for eyes. Thin curls of celery made antennae, and the body was bisected by an anchovy belt bordered on each side by thin lines of sliced pimiento. The mélange of flavors was as ludicrous as the looks of this creation.

The magazines and I have come a long way since then. While I was studying in France I encountered true French dressing and simple but elegant tossed green salads. Even tiny villages are able to bring forth such salads, the restaurants somehow acquiring the lettuces even in winter. I came to know why I had vaguely resented those salads in my childhood.

WHY SALADS STILL CAN FAIL

There are two outstanding flaws in most salads. The first is the use of bottled dressing of the red-menace type I spoke of. I have waged a losing one-man war against this in every restaurant I go to, and now I usually ask for Italian dressing, which is nearer to what the French use.

The other cause of failure is the casual way we treat the greens. Many people who are aware of what makes a good dressing still fail because they prevent the marriage of greens and dressing. My wife has become locally renowned for her salads, and although her dressings are certainly good, she feels the main reason she gets kudos is that she really *dries* the lettuce, literally dries every leaf. How can anyone expect oily dressing to adhere to a wet leaf? Has oil ever mixed with water? First of all you must have good greens—and these are not the kind of substitute-for-shoe-leather romaine supermarkets offer. Boston lettuce is much better than iceberg lettuce because the latter is so tightly headed you can never detach a leaf or properly dry it. If you grow your own, try 'Salad Bowl' and 'Butter-crunch' or 'Butter King.'

Wash the leaves thoroughly after they are pulled off the head. Put them in a wire salad basket and shake it vigorously to remove most of the water. Then take out the leaves and dry them with a linen towel or blot them dry with paper toweling. You can do this well in advance of the meal, put them in a fresh dry towel, and refrigerate them to keep them crisp. When you make the salad, tear them in bite-sized pieces and discard the pulpy part of the leaf rib.

One other note about dressing may be in order. Too many people overload the dressing with herbs, perhaps believing that if a half teaspoonful is good, a whole teaspoonful would be great. It isn't! Use restraint. And especially if you are using dried herbs, crumble them well between your fingers or pound them in a mortar. "Finely chopped" means just that with fresh herbs, and no big pieces or stems should be inflicted on your guests. After all, who wants to spend the evening picking pieces of oregano, let's say, out of his teeth? Mix your dressing well and mix it again just before use to ensure that it has not separated.

And finally, a tossed salad can mean either a violent love bout with the greens or a gentle tumbling, so long as every leaf gets covered with dressing and gleams as it is served. You too can become salad queen or salad master of your neighborhood if you work it right.

SALAD DRESSINGS

French Dressing
(Basic recipe is also called Sauce Vinaigrette)

1 cup olive oil
⅓ cup red wine vinegar
Salt and pepper to taste

Garlic, 1 clove halved
(optional)

Combine in a wide-mouthed jar with tight-sealing cover. Shake well, let stand at room temperature for 1 hour or longer, then remove garlic. Shake thoroughly before dressing salad greens. Yield: 1⅓ cups

VARIATIONS
These are almost legion, for everyone seems to have his own version. The classic one above is really from France and may, of course, be mixed in smaller quantities. The above quantity would be for a party salad. Keep 3-to-1 proportions of oil to vinegar, however the additives and other proportions may vary.

For economy's sake we usually use half olive and half Mazola oil, and the vinegar may also be varied to half red wine and half cider vinegar. Or the vinegar may be herbed vinegar (see p. 183), if the flavor is appropriate to the kind of food it is used with.

Herb additives: Marjoram, tarragon, mint, basil, chives, parsley, sage, and any other herb that will enhance the flavor of the salad or food it is used with. Many vegetable and fish dishes—asparagus, cauliflower, green beans, boiled fish, salmon, and so on—employ the classic French Sauce Vinaigrette, which is actually the French dressing above, with or without additional ingredients. Usually the sauce is poured over the vegetable or fish while it is hot or warm so that it may penetrate better into the food.

When marjoram, mint, and other dried herbs are added to French dressing for salads, be sure to pulverize the woody stems or remove them.

Italian Salad Dressing

½ *cup olive oil*
  3 *Tbs. wine vinegar (white*
    or red)

½ *tsp. dry mustard*
  1 *clove garlic, cut in half*
½ *tsp. salt*

Thoroughly mix salt, mustard, and garlic (mashing the clove in the process), add vinegar and stir well; add oil and again thoroughly mix. Allow to set in cool place a few hours, then remove garlic and it is ready for use.
Yield: about ⅔ cup

No-Oil Yoghurt Dressing

2 *hard-cooked eggs,*
  chopped
⅓ *cup yoghurt*
  3 *Tbs. cider vinegar*

½ *clove garlic, finely minced*
  8 *basil leaves, chopped*
  2 *tsps. parsley, finely*
    chopped

Put in blender container and blend at medium speed for 2 minutes or until smooth. This is a good dressing for fresh fruit salads. Tarragon may be substituted for parsley.
Yield: about ¾ cup

Creamy Cole Slaw Dressing

2 eggs
1 cup yoghurt
½ cup tarragon vinegar

1 Tb. honey
½ tsp. salt
1 tsp. celery seeds

Beat eggs well and combine with yoghurt in top of double boiler over hot water, adding other ingredients and stirring until mixture is smooth and somewhat thick. Cool before using. Other herb vinegars may be substituted.
Yield: about 1¾ cups.

Mayonnaise à la Blender

A godsend for the hard-pressed cook is the electric blender—a quick and efficient way to blend the ingredients for making a smooth mayonnaise and also to wed the flavors of herbs when you add them to the basic recipe here. It is important that all the ingredients be at room temperature to ensure success.

1 egg, unseparated
2 Tbs. vinegar (or lemon juice)
½ tsp. dry mustard

¾ tsp. salt
⅛ tsp. ground white pepper
1 cup oil (salad or olive)

In blender container put the egg, 1 tablespoon vinegar or lemon juice, salt, mustard, and pepper, and put cover on. Start blender at low speed (No. 2, if multiple-speed blender is used), and slowly pour in ½ cup oil while blending. Stop, make sure all ingredients are near the blades, add remaining 1 tablespoon vinegar

and ½ cup oil, and blend at high speed (No. 7, if multiple-speed).
Yield: 1 cup

NOTE
   Herbs may be added while blending first time, putting them in with the egg and other ingredients. Or see other recipes for various herb mayonnaise recipes.

Mustard Mayonnaise

1 pint mayonnaise (com-   2 tsps. dry mustard
   mercial or homemade)   2 tsps. distilled vinegar

Blend vinegar and mustard well in a bowl, then add mayonnaise and stir until completely blended. Refrigerate until time to serve. Good with fish—baked, broiled, or boiled.
Yield: 1 pint

Tarragon-Mustard Mayonnaise

1 tsp. oil   2 tsps. minced fresh tarragon
2 tsps. Dijon prepared   (or 1 tsp. dry tarragon)
   mustard   1 Tb. lemon juice
                               1 pint mayonnaise

Combine all ingredients except mayonnaise in a bowl and blend, being sure to break up dry tarragon, if used. Add mayonnaise and stir well until completely blended. Serve with fish and shellfish, fish mixtures for sandwiches, steaks, and veal scaloppine (add chopped parsley and *prosciutto* for this); in salads, espe-

cially chicken and fish salads; and mix with yolks for stuffed eggs.
Yield: 1 pint

Other Mayonnaises, Herb-Flavored

Nearly any herb can be mixed with mayonnaise, the herb(s) being chosen to go with the food the mayonnaise will be served with. Basil, oregano, and thyme, for instance may be mixed to go with egg dishes; basil added for anything with tomatoes in it, along with herbs to complement the other foods; and thyme with any other herb that goes well with fish and seafoods. Work out your own proportions, your own blends, adding herbs lightly until you achieve the ideal quantities.

Garlic-Nut Mayonnaise

From France, in that area west of the Rhône and north of Toulouse where Roquefort also delights the gourmet, comes this mayonnaise that is served with fish of all kinds.

4 bulbs garlic	*2 egg yolks*
⅓ cup hazelnuts (shelled,	*1½ cups olive oil*
toasted)	*⅛ tsp. black pepper, freshly*
1¼ cups shelled English	*ground*
walnuts	*1 Tb. lemon juice*
Salt	

Separate garlic cloves and peel them; toast hazelnuts and let cool. Pour boiling water over hazelnuts and walnuts and remove husks from them. In a mortar crush nuts and garlic with a little salt, add the egg yolks and mix well, then beat in the olive oil little by little. Add pepper and lemon juice when well mixed. Chill before serving.

Yield: about 1 cup

NOTE

This authentic recipe may prove too strong in garlic for many tastes, and we suggest that 6 to 8 cloves of garlic may be sufficient for a start. If you like a stronger taste, add more the next time you make it.

French Dressing à la Blender

French dressings may also be made in a blender, varying the taste with garlic salt, onion salt, wine vinegar or cider vinegar, or the various herb-flavored vinegars. Again, all ingredients must be at room temperature.

¼ cup vinegar (or lemon juice)
¾ cup oil (salad, olive, or half of each)
1 tsp. salt

¼ tsp. white or freshly ground black pepper
¼ tsp. sugar (optional)
Herbs, according to taste

Put all the ingredients into blender container, cover, and run at high speed (or No. 5) about 30 seconds.

Yield: 1 cup

NOTE

Herbs in season should be finely chopped. Our choice is mint, parsley, chives, marjoram, and for a tomato salad, basil. Often these can be combined. Dry herbs can be used also, but should be lightly pulverized in order to be absorbed and blended.

A Salad of Tossed Greens

The thing to remember is that a tossed green salad must be tossed—not merely tousled. That is the only way to be sure of coating each leaf with the dressing. Even then the greens will not be coated unless they are thoroughly dried before the dressing is added. For this one an oil-and-vinegar dressing—either wine or cider vinegar or half-and-half—with herbs to give it flavor, makes the mixed greens an admirable accompaniment for a luncheon, with a soup-and-salad Sunday-night supper, or a casserole entrée.

1 head Boston or other leaf
   lettuce
Other greens—endive,
   chicory, young spinach,
   dandelion, cress—to equal
   quantity of lettuce
1 clove garlic, cut in half

1 tsp. finely chopped fresh
   basil
1 tsp. finely chopped
   marjoram
1 tsp. chives, well chopped
1 tsp. finely chopped parsley

½ to ⅔ cup oil-and-vinegar dressing

Wash and thoroughly dry lettuce and other greens. (Any one or several of the greens may be added to the lettuce.) Tear or shred the lettuce and greens. Rub a wooden salad bowl with the cut garlic and discard the garlic. Mix salad dressing, add chopped herbs, and mix well. Add to greens in salad bowl and toss and toss until well coated.

Serves 4 to 6

VARIATIONS
   Fresh mushrooms or radishes, thinly sliced, or cucumber, peeled and sliced, may be added. Mushrooms are better with the blander greens—not with spinach or dandelions—which retain the full and delicate flavor of the raw mushroom.

Greek Salad

6 medium tomatoes, cut in
   small pieces
6 scallions, finely chopped
1 green pepper, coarsely
   chopped
1½ cups feta cheese, cubed
16 Greek olives, pitted
   (black, in oil)

Dressing:
   5 Tbs. olive oil
   2 Tbs. lemon juice
   1 to 2 cloves garlic
   ⅛ tsp. black pepper, freshly
     ground
Salt to taste
   ⅛ tsp. oregano (dried)
   1½ tsps. dried mint

Cut up tomatoes and drain, chop scallions and pepper, add cubed cheese. Pit olives and add.

Combine olive oil and lemon juice, press garlic and discard pulp, letting juice fall into olive-oil mixture. Add salt and pepper, oregano, and dried mint. Mix well, pour over salad ingredients and toss well.

Serves 6 to 8

NOTE

More garlic may be used if desired, and pitted jumbo black olives substituted if Greek olives are not obtainable.

Tomato Salad aux Fines Herbes

6 to 8 large tomatoes
2 Tbs. finely chopped basil
4 Tbs. finely chopped onion
1 or 2 cloves garlic, crushed
½ cup finely chopped parsley
2 Tbs. finely chopped
   tarragon (or 1 tsp. dried)

3 Tbs. red wine vinegar
6 Tbs. olive oil
Salt to taste
½ tsp. freshly ground black
   pepper
French salad dressing (p. 159)

166

Loosen skins of tomatoes by plunging briefly into boiling water. Peel, cut tomatoes evenly into ½-inch thick slices.

Make next nine ingredients into a rather thick dressing, mashing and mixing well together. Using about three-fourths of it, spread dressing between slices of tomato, building up to re-form tomato. Hold together with toothpicks. Chill.

Add remainder (one-quarter) of green mixture to French salad dressing and serve in a bowl, to be ladled over tomato when served. Put tomatoes on a bed of well-washed and -dried Boston or other leaf lettuce.

Serves 8

DESSERTS

Chocolate-Mint Omelet

Filling (2 servings):
¼ *cup semisweet chocolate*
   pieces
 1 *Tb. crème de menthe*
 2 *Tbs. heavy cream*
 1 *tsp. sugar*

Yield: about 6 tablespoons

Omelet (2 servings):
3 eggs, separated
2 tsps. instant coffee
 (optional)
2 Tbs. butter
4 tsps. very finely chopped
 mint
Sugar

Prepare filling first. (If more than two servings are to be made, increase recipe accordingly. Omelets are best made one at a time for each two servings.)

Melt chocolate in top of double boiler over hot, not boiling, water. Remove from heat and add crème de menthe, cream, and sugar, and stir in well. Cover and keep warm.

Make omelet. With a fork, blend egg yolks in a small bowl with coffee, if used. Beat egg whites in a medium-sized bowl until stiff peaks form. Fold in egg-yolk mixture with a rubber scraper until just blended with whites. Heat omelet pan and melt butter in it until it sizzles; do not let it brown. Add egg mixture quickly, spreading evenly over bottom of pan. Cook over medium heat until bottom is golden brown. Put omelet pan under broiler—about 6 inches below heat—for 2 minutes or until omelet top is golden brown.

Loosen edges with spatula and turn out on warm serving plate, top side down. Spoon 3 tablespoons filling in center and fold omelet in half. Sprinkle top with mint and sugar and drizzle 3 tablespoons filling over the top. Serve warm.

Yield: 1 omelet, 2 servings

Apple Crisp

Apples
½ cup all-purpose flour
1 cup dark-brown sugar
⅓ cup salt butter

3 Tbs. dried mint, crushed
½ cup Calvados or applejack
Whipped cream

Peel and slice enough apples to fill a buttered 2-quart casserole about two-thirds full. Blend in a bowl the flour, sugar, butter, and well-crushed or pulverized mint. Pour Calvados over apples in the casserole and top with the sugar mixture. Bake in a 375° F. oven until pudding is crisp and bubbly and apples are cooked through. Serve hot with whipped cream or a pitcher of heavy cream.

Serves 6 to 8

Apple Pie with Mint

Make pie according to your favorite recipe, but instead of the cinnamon usually called for, add ½ teaspoon mace, 1½ to 2 tablespoons lemon juice, 1 teaspoon grated lemon peel, and 2 tablespoons finely chopped mint.

Strawberry Delight

2 cups sliced strawberries
1 cup small-curd cottage
  cheese
2 to 3 Tbs. milk

2 Tbs. honey (or light-brown
  sugar)
4 tsps. finely chopped mint
Whole strawberries (garnish)

Wash and hull berries, slice and put in blender container with cottage cheese, honey, mint, and 2 tablespoons milk. Blend at low speed, then after 1 minute blend at high speed for a half minute. If very thick, add about 1 tablespoon more milk and blend briefly. Frozen strawberries may be used, thawing first and slicing if whole. If frozen berries are sugared, omit honey. Pour from blender into sherbet glasses or other dessert dishes and garnish each glass with a whole strawberry. Chill before serving.

Serves 6 to 8

NOTE
   The dessert may be prepared by putting berries and other ingredients through a sieve if a blender is not available.

Peach-Blueberry Cobbler

Peaches	Light-brown sugar
Blueberries	Vanilla
2 Tbs. chopped mint	Shortcake dough

Wash and pick over blueberries; drain. Peel and slice peaches and mix with blueberries; place in a deep baking dish, preferably square, to fill about two-thirds or a little more. (Quantities of all ingredients will vary with the size of dish.) Sprinkle mint and sugar generously over the top, add 1 teaspoon vanilla per 2 cups fruit. Top with shortcake dough and bake at 425° F. until topping is nicely brown and fruit tender. Serve either cold or hot with whipped cream.

Apple-Mint Charlotte

1½ cups boiling water	½ teaspoon vanilla
⅓ to ½ cup chopped mint	Thin toast
12 apples	¼ cup butter
Sugar	Vanilla ice cream

Pour boiling water over mint; simmer 10 minutes; strain and discard mint. Peel, quarter and core apples; cook in minted boiling water till soft; put in blender. Blend until puréed, measure; add equal amount of sugar and the vanilla. Return to heat and cook for about 15 minutes or until sauce is very thick. Melt butter, dip each slice of light, thin toast (crusts removed) in it, and brown on a griddle or skillet quickly. Line sides of a mold with toast, cutting it into shapes as necessary to fit contours so that mold is completely lined. If toast is too hard, dip quickly in milk to soften. Fill lined mold with applesauce, cover with soft-ened toast. Place mold in 1 inch of hot water in a pan and bake at 350° F. for 30 to 35 minutes. Toast must be solid enough to hold apple filling when unmolded.

Serve hot or cold with vanilla ice cream or whipped cream. Serves 6 to 8

Baked Apples

1 apple per serving
Sugar: about 2 Tbs. per apple
1 tsp. finely chopped mint
  per apple

1 Tb. butter per apple
Rum

Wash and core apples and peel top inch. Arrange in a baking dish. Mix sugar with mint and fill core cavities with mixture. Top each apple with 1 tablespoon butter. Fill baking dish with ½ inch water and bake in a preheated 350° F. oven for 30 minutes or until apples are tender, basting frequently with juices from the pan. Pour rum (cognac or Calvados may also be used) over apples when done, about 1 tablespoon for each 2 apples, and flambé, bringing the dish flaming to the table. Serve with mint-flavored whipped cream or custard.

VARIATIONS

1. Mix bread crumbs and raisins or chopped, pitted prunes in equal quantities with about 1 teaspoon chopped mint per apple, and fill core cavities. Again top with butter and flambé when done.

2. Finely chop peel of lemon, from which most of white por-tion has been pared. Mix ¼ teaspoonful with white raisins and 1 teaspoon chopped mint per apple and fill core cavities. Top with

171

butter, and when done and ready to serve, add 1 teaspoon dry sherry.

3. Mix half-and-half dark-brown sugar and well-crushed cornflakes with 1 teaspoon chopped mint per apple and pack in core cavities. Top with butter and bake.

Mint Syrup
(For Fruit Cups, Desserts, over Ice Cream)

¼ cup fresh mint leaves   *1 cup water*
Green coloring (optional)   *3 cups sugar*

Use only fresh and crisp mint leaves. Wash and dry lightly on paper towels. Put in saucepan and bruise lightly, then add water and cook over low heat for 3 minutes. Add sugar gradually, stirring to dissolve it. Bring to a boil on medium heat and allow to boil for 5 minutes. Remove from heat, let stand 10 minutes, then strain leaves out of syrup. Cool, put in bottle, and cork tightly.

Makes 1 cup

NOTE

Dried mint leaves may be used. Prepare as for herb tea, using 3 to 4 teaspoons mint to 1 cup boiling water. Cover and allow to steep for 5 minutes, then strain. Add 3 cups sugar to tea, bring to a boil, and allow to boil 5 minutes. Cool, bottle, and cork tightly.

Minted Strawberry Tarts

6 tart shells (2½ in.), baked
3 cups strawberries, crushed
1 Tb. lemon juice
2 Tbs. very finely chopped
   spearmint*

1 Tb. cornstarch
5 Tbs. sugar
Red coloring

Pick over and hull all strawberries, reserving best of small ones for tarts and 6 large ones. Mash and crush enough strawberries to make 3 cups and place in a saucepan with all other ingredients except reserved strawberries. Cook over low heat, stirring, until clear and thick. Cool for 5 to 10 minutes. Place several small whole strawberries in bottom of tart shells. Pour cooked berries over them. As the tarts cool put one large strawberry and two fresh mint leaves on top of each as decoration. Whipped cream may be served with them.
Serves 6

---

* Three tablespoons Mint Syrup, above, may be used in place of fresh mint. Decrease amount of sugar in recipe by 2 tablespoons.

Strawberry-Apple-Mint Pie

1 9-inch baked pie shell (or
   6 tart shells)
1 cup strawberries, crushed
2 medium apples, chopped
2 Tbs. finely chopped spearmint or apple mint*

1 cup water
1 cup sugar
Red coloring
Additional whole berries

Wash and hull berries; crush enough to make 1 cup. Reserve 6 or 8 berries of equal size for garnish and small ones to cover pie bottom. Pare and chop apples. In water in a saucepan dissolve sugar and add fruits and mint. Bring to a boil, then cook over low heat 5 minutes. Test for thickening, and when juice drops thickly off a spoon, remove from heat, stir in coloring, and cool for a few minutes. Arrange a layer of reserved berries over bottom of pie shell and pour warm mixture over them. Cool. As pie begins to set, place a berry on top for each serving, equidistant from each other and about halfway out from center. Whipped cream may be piped around berries or decorate the top as desired.

Makes 1 9-inch pie or 6 2½-inch tarts

---

* Three tablespoons Mint Syrup (p. 172) may be used in place of fresh mint. Decrease sugar by 2 tablespoons in the recipe.

Minted Strawberry Shortcake

According to some food historians, shortcake may possibly stem from French recipes for galettes, *which are somewhere between puff pastry and a pie or tart crust. These were served by the cooks with fruit jams or preserves between layers. Whatever its origin—and it is so thoroughly at home in America that it is useless to speculate—we have made it our own. Probably Americans added the whipped cream, and because we now have frozen strawberries (whole or sliced), we can enjoy it at any season, even though some of us feel that the fresh berries have a special flavor. My own addition is fresh mint, for its pungence combined with nonsweet shortcake counteracts the sweetness of sugared fruit. Probably my French forebears would approve, since they were adventurous enough to emigrate to America.*

The sickly sweet spongecake that in mediocre restaurants and even in some homes masquerades as "shortcake" is a far cry from the original, true (and truly short) shortcake.

SHORTCAKE

2 cups flour	1 Tb. sugar
4 tsps. baking powder	¾ cup milk
½ tsp. salt	¼ to ⅓ cup butter

Mix all dry ingredients and sift twice. Work in shortening with a pastry blender, and when smooth, add milk gradually. Blend it in thoroughly but gently.

Some cooks make one large round cake, some make 4-inch biscuits, and others divide the dough into two equal parts and flatten them on a floured board by patting with the hands to about ½-inch thickness. If making the latter, brush both liberally with melted butter, then place one of them on top. On a lightly greased cookie sheet bake 15 to 20 minutes at 400° F. Remove from oven, open halves, and brush both with butter. Cool. Just before serving fill.

STRAWBERRY FILLING

1 quart dead-ripe	2 cups heavy cream
strawberries*	Candied mint leaves (p. 178;
½ cup sugar	optional)
¼ cup finely chopped mint	
leaves	

Rinse off and hull strawberries. Reserve about half, selecting the most perfect berries of similar size. Cut the rest in half and place in a bowl, sprinkling with half the sugar. Put the mint in bowl with the berries. Put whole berries in another bowl and sprinkle with remaining sugar. Chill. Whip cream, sweeten, and chill. Just before serving, open shortcake, cover lower half with cut berries, and drizzle the juice over all. Put the other half on and spoon the whipped cream over it. Arrange whole berries in the cream in an even pattern, using candied mint leaves with each berry. Or cut all berries in the beginning, add mint, and put sugar with them in a bowl. Cover bottom half of shortcake with berries, then put remaining berries over the top, and spoon whipped cream over all.

Serves 8

---

* Raspberries may be substituted for strawberries.

Minted Strawberry Meringue Torte

The same method of slicing strawberries and adding mint and sugar may be employed for this delectable dessert. Less sugar may be used, since the meringues are quite sweet. And, again, raspberries may be used instead of strawberries, combining them with 2 tablespoons chopped mint.

6 eggs, separated	2 Tbs. lemon juice, strained
½ tsp. cream of tartar	(optional)
1¾ cups fine sugar	2 cups heavy cream
2 tsps. grated lemon peel	2 Tbs. powdered sugar XXX
(optional)	

Beat egg whites until stiff, and gradually add cream of tartar and sugar; continue beating until whites stand in stiff peaks.

In electric mixer: Beat egg whites in small bowl at high speed for 3 minutes, then add sugar gradually and lemon ingredients (see note) while continuing to beat at high speed until mixture stands up in stiff peaks, about 4 to 5 minutes.

Pencil two circles the desired size (9 to 10 inches) on a piece of heavy brown paper. Heavily grease it. Shape the torte on these circles with a spatula or spoon and bake in a preheated oven at 250° F. for 1½ hours. Turn off oven, open door a little, and leave torte in oven to crisp for an hour or until ready to serve. Meringues may be soft to touch at first and therefore should be left to crisp.

To serve, remove torte layers carefully from paper and place on plate, filling layers with strawberry mixture (p. 175), spooning whipped cream over each layer. Top with whipped cream and whole strawberries as for Strawberry Shortcake.

Serves 10 to 12

NOTE

Lemon peel and juice may be omitted for raspberry torte.

SWEET HERB SAUCES

Minted Pineapple Sauce for Desserts

¼ *cup chopped mint (or 1½
  Tbs. dried)*
½ *cup honey*
¾ *cup pineapple juice (from
  can)*

Green food coloring
*1 cup canned crushed
  pineapple*

Simmer liquid (add water if juice from crushed pineapple is not enough) with honey and mint for 10 to 15 minutes, stirring to prevent catching on. Strain to remove mint, then add green coloring a drop at a time until color is suitable. Add pineapple and simmer 5 minutes longer. Cool and chill. Use for sweet sauces on desserts, ice cream, cake, puddings, and dessert crêpes.

Yield: about 1¾ to 2 cups

Hot Citrus-Mint Sauce

2 Tbs. grated lemon rind
2 Tbs. grated orange rind
½ cup lemon juice
½ cup orange juice
½ cup chopped mint leaves
    (or 3 to 4 Tbs. dried)

2 Tbs. light-brown sugar
⅛ tsp. salt
⅛ tsp. paprika (optional)
¼ tsp. nutmeg (ground)

Combine all ingredients in top of double boiler. Set over barely boiling water for 30 minutes, stirring often as it cooks. Strain through a sieve, if desired, or serve as is. Good with roast lamb, game birds, turkey, and chicken.

Yield: about 1¼ to 1½ cups

Candied Mint Leaves for Desserts

1 cup fresh mint leaves
1 egg white, beaten

½ tsp. water
Granulated sugar

Pick mint in early morning, wash in cold water. Remove leaves from stem, press dry on paper towels, and select perfect leaves. To egg white add water and beat well but not stiff. Dip leaves in egg to coat both sides thoroughly, then dip in sugar to cover entire leaf surface. Place on waxed paper to dry for a day or two. Or, for quick drying, put waxed paper on a cookie sheet, coat leaves, allow to dry for an hour or two, and then put the cookie sheet in a preheated 200° F. oven, turn off heat and leave door partly open. When oven has completely cooled, leaves are ready to store.

Store in a tin box or other container that can be tightly closed. On waxed paper put leaves in layers nearly touching, and seal box or cover tightly. Use leaves to decorate desserts, cakes, ice cream, icings, with fresh or preserved fruit, on whipped cream, and wherever the taste of mint and the leaf as decoration would be appropriate.

NOTE

Herb flowers and other simple flowers may be preserved. Borage blossoms, rose petals, and any other edible flowers, such as violets, may be similarly treated.

MISCELLANEOUS

Bouquets Garnis

These are flavoring agents composed of several herbs—a sprig or two of each—in various combinations, tied together and immersed in liquids of such dishes as stews, soups, and certain vegetables at some point early in the process of cooking. They are removed before the dish is finally served. White thread should be used for tying. Another method is to place the tied herbs in a cheesecloth bag, making retrieval of all portions of the herbs easier and more certain.

Select fresh young sprigs, cut them in the morning, and wash them thoroughly under cold running water, then tie together. Various combinations lend a variety of flavors to the dishes they are used in. It is possible, to make several *bouquets garnis* at the same time and thus save time in the future as well as taking advantage of herbs that are at their best. Put them in plastic bags, make sure to identify them with a label, and freeze them for later use.

Here are a few useful combinations:

* 1 sprig parsley, 1 sprig basil, 2 small green onions
* 2 sprigs parsley, 1 sprig thyme
* 2 sprigs parsley, 1 sprig marjoram, 6 to 8 chive leaves
* 1 sprig parsley, 1 small stalk celery with leaves, 6 chive leaves
* 1 sprig parsley, 1 sprig tarragon (small), 6 chive leaves
* 1 small sprig marjoram, 1 celery stalk with leaves, 6 chive leaves
* 2 sprigs parsley, 2 sprigs spearmint, 1 sprig thyme, 8 chive leaves

Fines Herbes

The French phrase *fines herbes*, which occurs in many recipes, means merely a mixture of herbs. It is used in flavoring and seasoning soups, stews, egg dishes such as omelettes, and so on. Traditionally it means simply a mixture of chopped parsley, chervil, chives, and tarragon, or some combination of these; but there are many variations and each chef has his own "secret" mixture. The *fines herbes* may be composed of fresh, frozen-and-thawed, or dried herbs. Many cooks make up their own blends when harvesting the herbs and freeze the mixture in plastic bags, ready for instant use.

Here are some useful combinations.

Fines Herbes, Classic Blend

1 Tb. chopped chives　　　　*3 tsps. chopped parsley*
1 tsp. chopped chervil　　　　*½ tsp. chopped tarragon*
(optional)

Select fresh young leaves, wash well, dry on towels, paper, or absorbent cotton. Mince well with a sharp knife. If chervil is unobtainable, add its quantity in parsley. Use mixture for flavoring meat, vegetables, soups, stews, or as filling for an omelette. Or garnish fish, roasts, or steaks with it, sprinkling lightly over all just before serving.

Fines Herbes, Blend for Vegetables

3 Tbs. dried mint　　　　*1 tsp. celery seed*
3 Tbs. dried sage　　　　*1 tsp. white pepper*

Rub through a fine sieve or pound to powder in a mortar. Pack in a dark bottle or other tightly sealed container. Use mixture to season boiled carrots, cauliflower, peas, string beans, and other sweet vegetables. Use ¼ to ½ teaspoonful for recipes that serve 4 to 6.

Fines Herbes, Meat and Sauce Blend

1 Tb. basil
1 Tb. marjoram
1 Tb. parsley

1 Tb. winter savory
    (optional)
1 Tb. thyme
1 tsp. lemon peel

Use dried leaves, discarding any stems that may be in the dried-leaf mixture, and blend thoroughly. Pulverize leaves in a mortar or pound well in a shallow bowl. Lemon peel should be pulverized separately before adding and mixing into herb mixture. Put through a fine sieve, then store in a dark bottle or other tightly sealed container. Use to flavor meat sauces, soups, vegetable and meat casseroles. Add ¼ to ½ teaspoon to recipes that serve 4 to 6.

Fines Herbes, Meat Blend

1 Tb. marjoram
1 Tb. parsley
1 Tb. sage
1 Tb. savory (optional)

1 Tb. thyme
1 Tb. celery seed
1 Tb. lemon peel

Use dried leaves, discarding any stems in the dried-leaf mixture; blend thoroughly. Pulverize leaves in a mortar or pound well in a shallow bowl. Separately pulverize celery seed and lemon peel before adding and mixing with herb mixture. Store in two or three dark bottles tightly sealed to keep flavor intact. Use what is needed and promptly replace sealing cap. Use ½ teaspoon for recipes that serve 6. Sprinkle lightly over beef or veal steaks, beef or pork roasts, and also use to flavor meat-base soups, stews, and ragouts.

Herb Vinegars

Much is made of the role of vinegar in salad dressings, and rightly so. The piquancy of vinegar and the blandness of the oil makes the salad dressing memorable, one way or another. Too much vinegar and the dressing will be sharp; too little and there is no zest to the salad. One way to bring out flavors in various salads is to use an herb vinegar, and these are quite easy to make. The purists insist on the classic way of adding vinegar to herb leaves and letting it stand in a warm place 10 to 14 days (and some advocate setting the tightly stoppered bottle in the sun, while others swear by no sun at all); and the argument about what sort of vinegar to use also has never been settled. White distilled or white wine vinegar is mostly the choice of gourmets, who cite the fact that cider vinegar has too much flavor of its own. Also, cider vinegar may have a bit of color that is not wanted in pale dressings. All that is open to individual choice, but the one thing everyone agrees on is that if the vinegar is to be heated, a porcelained or stainless steel pot should be used, for other metals may react to the acid in the vinegar, imparting unwanted flavors.

A simple way, and quick too, is a French method. It is practical, efficient, and ideal for home use. Pick fresh, mature leaves of herbs and measure them according to the recipe. Gently bruise them before putting them in the pan. Vinegar (the French use either white wine or red wine vinegar) is poured over them and brought quickly to a boil. At this point the heat is turned off, the pot covered, and the vinegar allowed to cool. When cool, it is strained and bottled, tightly corked or sealed, and stored. Most people put a leaf or two—even a sprig—in a bottle, and if you make herb vinegars for gifts, this is a decorative way to make the bottle distinctive.

For those who are choosing herbs to use, the following lists may be helpful. We take no sides in the cider-vs-distilled-vs-wine controversy.

With white wine or distilled vinegar: Basil, chives, garlic, marjoram, mint, onion, spearmint, tarragon, and thyme.

With red wine: Basil, chives, garlic, tarragon, thyme.

With cider vinegar: Basil, chives, garlic, marjoram, mint, onion, spearmint, tarragon, thyme.

Herb vinegars can be made with dried herbs too, preferably using the heated vinegar method. As a guide, the general rule is that ½ teaspoon dried herb equals 2 scant teaspoons of fresh, minced herb; ¼ teaspoon pulverized herb equals 2 scant teaspoons of fresh, minced herb.

An herbed vinegar can be used in making mayonnaise, avoiding the flecks of herb leaf, if either the fresh or dried herbs are used, that might appear in the finished product. For mayonnaise as for salads a general guide would be to choose the herb suited to the kind of food it is to be used with.

Herb Butters

Flavored butter is an interesting and useful way to bring herb taste to foods. It is simple to make and can be quickly prepared and used. It is usual to employ unsalted sweet butter, although some cooks use salted butter or even margarine, and I have heard of chicken fat being used in the same way. Herb butters may be melted on broiled meats and fish, on vegetables, boiled or poached eggs, and combined with bread crumbs for a richer crumb mixture where this is indicated or desirable in a recipe.

The usual proportions are 1 stick (¼ lb.) butter to 1 tablespoon minced fresh herb (less for the stronger herbs, perhaps), and 1 teaspoon lemon juice. When dried herbs are used, they should be pulverized or at least crumbled, and if they are soaked in the lemon juice for a quarter to a half hour before mixing with butter, the flavor will be enhanced. Fresh herbs are also ground in a mortar before being blended thoroughly with the softened, creamed butter. Allow to stand at room temperature for at least an hour—two is better—before use or before placing in a tightly covered small container for storage in the refrigerator. The butter may be kept for a week or so under refrigeration.

HERBS PARTICULARLY GOOD IN BUTTERS

Fresh herbs: Gather tender young leaves or tips of shoots at the time they are most flavorful (see harvesting, Chapter VI) and wash in cold water; gently blot dry on paper towels.

Dried herbs: A general rule is to use ⅓ or ¼ amount of dried herbs to proportion for fresh herbs. Because 1 tablespoon equals 3 teaspoons, therefore, use 1 teaspoon or less of dried herb.

Basil, chives, dill and dill seed, garlic, mint, oregano (and to a lesser degree marjoram), parsley, rosemary, sage, tarragon, and thyme are all useful in one way or another in herb butters. And combinations of herbs may also be employed where the flavors are called for or desirable. Tarragon and savory, thyme and parsley, chives and parsley, dill and garlic, are all good; and parsley may be combined half-and-half with Dijon mustard for a piquant butter for steaks, egg dishes, and certain fish and meats.

Herbed Bread Crumbs

Bread crumbs for dressings, various stuffings, and for use in breading for deep frying, crumbs called for to top some desserts and for any other recipe can be prepared ahead of time and stored for short periods to long periods, according to the ingredients.

To make crumbs: chop up bits of bread in a blender or by hand, drying in a slow oven until thoroughly dried out. If hand chopped, crumbs may be chunky and large. To make them finer, dry and place between sheets of waxed paper or foil and roll with a rolling pin. Measure 2 cups crumbs and put in a bowl. Dried herbs may be more easily sprinkled than fresh herbs, but if fresh herbs are finely minced, they may be distributed fairly evenly in mixing. Over the crumbs sprinkle herb or herbs, lightly distributing about half the amount. With a fork toss and mix herbs well, then sprinkle remaining herbs, and again mix until all crumbs are well mixed with herbs.

Where buttered crumbs are indicated, butter can be melted and herbs combined with it, then crumbs added and quickly mixed over low heat. Or heat can be turned off and crumbs mixed in cooling herb butter.

Herbed Garlic Butter

1 clove garlic, finely minced	2 tsps. finely minced
1/2 cup butter	fresh parsley
1 tsp. dried basil	1 green onion, finely
1/2 tsp. dried thyme	chopped (omit top)
1/4 tsp. dried tarragon	1/4 tsp. grated lemon peel

Dash cayenne pepper   Pinch salt (optional)

Crush garlic in a mortar. Mix butter with dried herbs, parsley and onion in bowl, adding lemon peel, cayenne, and salt (if butter is salted, salt is optional). When well blended, add to garlic and mix thoroughly. Chill until time to use, then heat and serve over vegetables—carrots, green beans, cauliflower, broccoli—or with broiled steak.

This may also be used instead of usual garlic butter on French bread. Slice loaf as usual—not entirely through—and brush each slice with butter, or soften butter (but do not heat) and spread on slices. Place loaf in a 400° F. oven to warm for 10 minutes or wrap loaf in foil and leave 15 to 20 minutes to warm and allow garlic butter to permeate.

Yield: ½ cup

Herb Marinade for Beef Burgundy and Other Meats

3 cups red burgundy   ¼ tsp. pulverized rosemary
½ cup brandy   1 tsp. salt
1 large onion, sliced thinly   15 peppercorns, cracked
Bouquet garni*

Mix the marinade well, place meat in a large flat bowl, and pour the marinade over it. Cover the bowl; turn the meat occasionally to bring all parts into contact with the marinade, which should permeate the meat thoroughly. Marinate for 6 hours or overnight in cool spot or refrigerator.

---

* **Bouquet garni:** A sprig each of parsley, basil, and if available, savory; combine with 2 small stalks celery with leaves. Bruise leaves before adding to wine mixture to release flavor.

Herb-Flavored Jellies

Lamb with mint jelly is well known, but other jellies are less common. Herbs give a special tang to ordinary apple jelly. In addition to the mints—spearmint, peppermint, curly mint, apple mint, and so on—jellies flavored with rosemary, sage, thyme, basil, and tarragon are also possible. A recipe for making jellies is usually included with the bottle or package of pectin, the jelling agent, for guidance. Pectin is available at supermarkets, groceries, and various food markets.

Basic Apple Jelly

5 lbs. tart, acid apples   *Sugar, oven-warmed*
5 cups cold water

Wash apples and quarter, leaving peel and cores intact. Place in a saucepan with a cover, add water, and cook, covered, over medium heat until apples are tender, about 20 to 25 minutes. Pour into a jelly bag and let drip until well drained. Do not press bag or jelly will not be clear. Measure the strained juice and note number of cups, since for each cup ¾ cup of sugar will be needed. Heat the juice and add warmed sugar gradually. Bring to a rapid boil and cook until it reaches 222° F. or sheets from a silver spoon, or other jelly tests show it is ready. Skim, then pour hot into sterilized hot glasses. Cover immediately with melted paraffin to seal. Four cups of juice are considered a proper batch to cook at one time.
Yield: about 2 pints of jelly

Mint Essence

1 cup chopped mint leaves and stems   *Boiling water*

Use tightly packed measure for mint; bruise leaves and stems. Pour boiling water over all, barely covering mint. Stir and press leaves into hot water. Allow to steep and cool for 6 to 8 hours. Strain, pressing leaves firmly with a spoon to extract all possible flavor and juice.

To flavor apple jelly, use 2 to 4 tablespoons mint essence per pint of hot apple juice, adding just before sugar is added. Jelly will not be green, but a light pinkish color. Green vegetable coloring may be added, drop by drop, if desired. Cork and store unused essence for later use.

Other Methods

If you do not wish to make essence, mint leaves or sprigs of basil can be put in the saucepan with the apples and boiled for the last 3 or 4 minutes of cooking. Strain them out when straining apple pulp. Or 4 or 5 sprigs can be placed in the hot strained apple juice for 3 to 4 minutes, then removed before sugar is added. If basil is used, leave only 2 to 3 minutes.

Thyme, rosemary, sage, and tarragon are all best prepared as essence. Since they are strong-flavored, use only a half cup of leaves for essence. Add 1 tablespoon essence per pint of jelly, taste, and add a little more if you wish a more definite flavor.

Rosemary Pectin Jelly

⅓ to ½ cup dried rosemary   3 cups sugar
2 cups boiling water   ½ bottle liquid pectin (3 oz.)
2 Tbs. lemon juice, strained

Pour boiling water over rosemary, cover, and let infuse for 1 to 2 hours. Strain, put in saucepan over high heat, add lemon juice and sugar; stir. When boiling point is reached, add pectin and boil for 1 minute. Remove from heat and pour immediately into hot sterilized glasses and seal with hot paraffin.
Yield: about 1 pint

General and Horticultural Index

(*For the convenience of the cook, an Index of Recipes begins on page 199.*)

Aerosol sprays, 65
Agro-Lite, 71
Alcohol, for mealybugs, 65
Alkaline soil, 60
Allium schoenoprasum (chives), 16–17
Anethum graveolens (dill), 18–19
Aphids, 65
Artemisia dracunculus (tarragon), 36–38
Artificial light, *see* Light garden
Anise, 9
Annuals, care of, 55
Apple mint (*Mentha rotundifolia*), 23–24
American (*M. gentilis* var. *variegata*), 24
Aromatic teas, *see* Teas

Barbarea vulgaris (garden cress), 43
Basil (*Ocimum basilicum*), 14–15
culture, 15, 61 (chart)
keeping qualities, 81
recipes for using (list), 15
Béarnaise sauce, tarragon in, 37
Beef, *see* Meats
Bergamot mint (*Mentha citrata*), 45

Beverages, herbs for flavoring, 23, 40, 43, 44, 45
Bouquets garnis, 11, 17
drying, freezing, 76
see also Index of Recipes
Burpee's Curlycress, 43
Butters, herbs used in, 185
Butter sauce, tarragon in, 37

Calendula officinalis (pot marigold), 44
Catnip (*Nepeta cataria*), 43
Cheeses, herbs with, 21, 23, 34, 40, 43
Chervil, 81
Chives (*Allium schoenoprasum*), 16–17
culture, 16–17, 61 (chart)
drying, freezing, 77
keeping qualities, 81
recipes using (list), 17
"Chive salt," 16
Chlorine, removing from water, 61–62
Chrysanthemum balsamita (costmary), 43
Cinnamon, 9
Clay pots, 56, 58
see also Pots and containers

191

Index of Recipes